DR. BADER'S PEST CURES

NATURAL SOLUTIONS
To
BIGGER PESTS

BY

DR. MYLES H. BADER

NEW ILLUSTRATIONS

FOR EASIER IDENTIFICATION

IF THEY ARE FLYING, CRAWLING, BURROWING OR SNEAKING
IN, THIS BOOK HAS THE natural SOLUTION

THIS BOOK WILL PROVIDE THE METHOD OF
ELIMINATING ALMOST ANY INSECT

OR CRITTER PROBLEM - NATURALLY!

NATURAL SOLUTIONS TO BIGGER PESTS

By
Dr. Myles H. Bader

NOTE:
Some substances in this book can be harmful if not used with caution. Please avoid disregarding precautions or breathing in or ingesting the ingredients. When working with any chemical it is always advisable to wear a protective mask and/or rubber gloves. Many, but not all, of the solutions in this book are harmless to humans and pets. The information provided in this book is for educational and entertainment use only. You accept full responsibility for any use of this information, which is provided "as is" without any representations or warranties whatsoever. Telebrands Corp. ("Publisher") is not responsible for any errors or omissions. Publisher shall not be liable, in contract, tort, or otherwise, to the reader or any other entity or individual for any personal or property injury, loss of profits, direct, indirect, special, punitive, consequential, special or incidental loss or damage, of any nature whatsoever.

TELEBrands **PRESS**

Fairfield, NJ 07004

A WORD ABOUT THE AUTHOR

Dr. Myles H. Bader known as the "Wizard of Food" as well as the "Buggy Professor" has been a prolific writer of kitchen reference, household hint and cooking secret books for over 17 years. Dr. Bader is also a recognized leader in the field of preventive care, weight management, nutrition and wellness and has been a guest on over 6,000 radio talk shows and 135 television shows including Oprah, The Discovery Channel, America's Talking, HGTV, QVC, Trinity Broadcasting, Fox & Friends, NBC and Help at Home.

Dr. Bader received his Professional Medical Degree from Loma Linda University and is board certified as a Preventive Care Practitioner. He is experienced in weight control, exercise physiology, stress management, early detection of heart disease, has counseled in all areas of nutrition and has lectured extensively on supplementation and anti-aging for 30 years. He has also established multi-phasic screening prevention programs for numerous safety departments, city governments and executive health programs for over 40 major corporations.

Dr. Bader has authored 23 books including "The Encyclopedia of Kitchen & Cooking Secrets." "Cookbook's Companion," "1,001 All-Natural Secrets to a Pest-Free Property" "20,001 Food Secrets, Chefs Secrets & Household Hints," "The Wellness Desk Reference," "1,001 Secret Household Formulas & Money Saving Tips," "10,001 Food Facts, " "To Supplement or Not to Supplement," "Grandmother's Kitchen Wisdom" and many more. Dr. Bader's books have formally been marketed by; Barnes & Noble, Amazon, Reader's Digest, Book of the Month Club and Doubleday.

TABLE OF CONTENTS

INTRODUCTION

TOXIC CHEMICALS
The use of toxic chemicals is really taking the "easy way out!" Our grandparents and great grandparents managed to grow flower gardens and vegetables long before the invention of pesticides. They knew how to control and eliminate the critters and chase them away without poisoning the environment, your surroundings and the ground water.

There is presently about 3 billion pounds of synthetic pesticides manufactured in the United States annually, which is one-quarter of the world's total. The EPA has recognized the problem and has stated that the pesticides are a major threat to groundwater in all areas of the country.

The sad fact is that 67% of all pesticides are thought to cause cancer in humans and pets. When trying to get rid of those pests we need to learn to eliminate them naturally instead of putting ourselves and the planet at risk. Remember, the poison you are using on the garden pest can kill you and your pets as well!

PUBLIC AWARENESS
The public needs to become more aware of the dangers involved from using toxic chemicals and start using a more natural approach to getting rid of critter pests. While many of the methods mentioned in this book provides ways of ridding your property of the pest without killing them, a number of the methods, even though they are all-natural may harm certain small critters that burrow underground.

There are natural methods of dealing with almost any type of critter but the information has been difficult to obtain until now. The information in this book is accurate and very effective. Hundreds of the facts have been handed down for hundreds of years long before pest control services and toxic products became popular and had harmful chemical cures.

In 2011 more than 3.8 million people suffered medically related side effects from the use of pesticides. Some of the immediate effects included dizziness, nausea, headaches and loss of energy.

This book has been designed to make it easy to find the information you need and the answers to your questions are very precise. If any substances are recommended they will be easy to locate, and easy to assemble into a usable controlled substance. Always try the simplest method first before going to a stronger one. Some of the stronger methods may harm many of the beneficial insects and even some animals.

The author assumes no responsibility for any damage to plants, animals or people from the use of any solution or formulas given in this book. Care should be taken when spraying or using any harmful chemicals. Even though almost all the formulas are prepared from natural ingredients some may still be poisonous or cause illness and should be kept away from pets and children. When using powders of any type, it is best to wear a mask.

IDENTIFYING YOUR PROBLEM

Before trying to remove the pests and critters from your garden or yard, you must first identify the type of pest you are dealing with. This may not be easy since there are many pests that will do similar damage to your plants or property making it hard to find out which pest is guilty.

It is first necessary to study the damage and solve the mystery. If the plants leaves are full of holes or have been chewed, the type of hole or damaged area and its shape may give you a clue. The plant may be cut off at the base and pulled underground by a burrowing critter. The leaves may be chewed around the edges or there may be a small hole in the stem or root vegetable. Was the damage done during the day or during the night?

CONTROLLING YOUR OUTSIDE SURROUNDINGS

There are a number of ways that a gardener can control the surroundings to deter pests. Crop rotation will enrich the soil, which is one method of controlling certain species. The rule of thumb is 3 years for large crops and 6 years for small gardens. You can also plant deterrents that repel the critters.

CONTROLLING YOUR INSIDE SURROUNDINGS

Prevention is the best method to keep pests from entering your house. Be sure all openings to the outside are sealed with proper materials such as a steel wool pad. Keep counters clean and occasionally wash with vinegar and water, food should be properly stored and never left out, trash containers inside and outside need to have a tight lid and if possible, kept off the ground.

CHAPTER 1

DEER

DEER

General Information:

 On the average a deer consumes about 5 pounds of greenery every day. Their diet consists of stems, leaves and buds of woody plants, however, their diet will vary depending on the food source available. They are creatures of habit and will return to the same general vicinity every day. Deer especially like to eat roses, but will settle for corn or grains and will usually not eat grasses.

Deer are ruminants or cud-chewers and have a four-chambered stomach. The teeth of deer are very well adapted to feeding on vegetationand like other ruminants they lack upper incisors, instead having a tough pad at the front of their upper jaw. The cheek teeth of deer have crescent ridges of enamel, which enable them to grind a wide variety of vegetation.

There are a number of methods of deterring deer without harming them. It is best to use a non-toxic method that does not have to be applied after every rain. However, if the rain is very heavy it will be necessary to re-apply a deterrent. Once a deterrent is used the deer will go to another area to forage and you may not have to spray again.

There are 38 different species of deer, however, the deer family. The deer family also includes elk, moose, caribou and reindeer. The most common found in North America belong to the genus Odocoileus. This includes Odocoileus virginianus - white-tailed deer, Odocoileus columbianus - The black-tailed deer, Odocoileus hemionus - The mule deer, Alces alces – moose and Cervus elaphus - The Red Deer or called Elk.

DEER FACTS:
- ➢ The male deer is referred to as a stag or a buck
- ➢ The offspring, or a baby deer, is a fawn or yearling
- ➢ The female deer is called a doe or hind
- ➢ The average size of a litter is one or two fawns
- ➢ The collective name for a group of deer is a herd
- ➢ The sound made by a deer is called a bellow
- ➢ Fully grown male deer reach the height of 7 feet

- The smallest member of the deer family is the pudu, which is a native of the Andes in Chile and is only 13-inches tall
- Deer have very compact bodies with long, powerful legs
- Deer are excellent swimmers
- Deer mark their territory by leaving a strongly scent
- Deer weights generally range from 70 to 700 ponds

NATURAL SOLUTIONS

BIRD NETTING WORKS GREAT!
Stretch the bird netting over a framework of PVC pipe painted green and use it over raised bed planters. The deer apparently don't see as well as they hear and smell and poke their nose into the netting, which startles them and they run away scared. However, there is nothing protruding through the netting or it will be eaten. Just roll the netting back if you wish to work in the area.

NATURAL FERTILIZER WORKS GREAT
Purchase small drawstring bags made of muslin or cheesecloth and fill them with Milorganite, an organic fertilizer that is safe around kids and pets, however, use with caution. Hang the bags on bushes, trees and shrubs the deer frequent.

DEER DETERRENT
The following ingredients will be needed:

1	Tablespoon of cayenne pepper
3	Tablespoons of kelp
3	Tablespoons of liquid hand soap
½	Teaspoon of oil of peppermint
1	Pint of warm water

Place all the ingredients into a medium bowl and mix well. Be careful not to get the cayenne pepper in your eyes. Place the mixture into a spray bottle and spray the areas where the deer frequent. *Do not use on plants that you will be consuming.*

STICKY SOLUTION
Mix 1 large egg in a quarter cup of tap water and mix well. The mixture is placed into a spray bottle and sprayed on the tree or plants. This is fine for a small area and the egg mixture is sticky enough to withstand a light rain without being re-applied.

CLOTHS & RAGS MAY DO THE TRICK!
Try hanging fabric softener sheets every 3 feet from branches or you can try ammonia-soaked rags, which work well.

HAVE A LICK OR TWO
Set out a new salt lick for the deer and the deer will stray from their normal path for this new salt lick. This has been very effective for a number of farmers. Set out salt licks quite a ways away from the garden and the deer will make a new path and bypass the garden on their nightly stroll.

MAKE WATER AND EGG OMELET SPRAY
Here's a cheap and environmentally safe solution! Mix one slightly beaten egg with 1 quart of water, place the mixture in a spray bottle and spray onto anything that the deer eat. This will have to be re-applied about every 4-5 days or after a rain but it is very effective.

URINE TO GO
Some farmer's supply stores sell coyote urine, such as Agway. Some stores have different kinds of urine and this is very effective keeping almost all critters away, except coyotes!

HERBAL COMBINATION
The combination of the following herbs mixed together works wonders on most animals, especially deer; black pepper, cayenne pepper, garlic and curry powder. Be sure and spray a small amount of water around the are to be sure it sticks to the ground.

SMELLY SOLUTION IN EXTREME CASES

The scent of humans is repulsive to most wild animals and marking your territory with your scent is a natural deterrent. However, it is a bit unorthodox but if you save some urine and sprinkle it in the areas the deer frequent, it will work 100% effective. You can also soak some rags in a bucket of some urine (using plastic gloves of course) then bury them at the outside rim of your garden with some mulch.

MAKE THEM AN OMELET

For a large area mix 1 cup of whole milk, 2 large eggs 2 tablespoons of canola oil, 2 tablespoons of Ivory Liquid Soap™ into 2 gallons of cool water. This mixture is very effective and is normally used in a spray bottle.

HAIR, HERE

Offer to sweep up the hair for your local beauty or barbershop, keep the hair and spread a small amount around the areas you are having trouble in. The human scent will keep deer away for some time or at least until it rains 2-3 times. You can place the hair into old socks and hang them from the tree. Using dirty gym socks works really great and will probably keep the neighbors away as well.

SAVE THE USED SOAP

Small bars of used soap can be hung from trees and bushes that deer eat. The human smell on the bar of soap tends to keep them away. Small bags of blood meal hung on the trees will accomplish the same thing. You can also use soap flakes instead of bars of soap placed in old stockings.

A REAL STINKER

The smell of rotten eggs is very offensive to many animals, especially deer. When eggs go bad they give off hydrogen sulfide and that really stinks bad. Deer will never come anywhere near an area that smells that bad. This is not a good deterrent to use too near your home.

NOT A HINDRANCE

Try purchasing a gallon of Hinder™, which is highly recommended by garden supply companies. It is made from a special concoction using capsaicin and only takes about 5 ounces to 2 gallons of water. However, you need to spray for 3 days straight and is especially good on roses.

SOUNDS FISHY

This is a sure-fire deer deterrent if you want to go through the trouble. For a small area it really works well but is mainly used on large flower farms or by people with really big areas near a national forest. Mix together 3 tablespoons of finely ground kelp with 1 cup of smelly fish emulsion and throw in 3 tablespoons of Ivory Liquid Soap™. Add enough water to make it easy to spray, then spray directly on the plants or trees.

A BLOODY DETERRENT

The following ingredients will be needed:

1	**Tablespoons of dried blood (garden supply house)**
4	**Cloves of powdered garlic**
2	**Gallons of cool tap water**

Place the water into a bucket and add the dried blood, then mix well. Place a portion into a sprayer and spray the area that the deer frequent. Use sparingly, since this formula is high in nitrogen and may burn plants. It also works great to keep rabbits away!

CHIVES TO THE RESCUE

Line each flower bed or vegetable garden with chives! It works great and you will have flowers all season, but you have to stay on top of the chives or they can take over the garden.... but when you weed the garden you can just weed out some of the chives as well.

DEER-OFF

There is an excellent natural deer repellant called Deer-off™. It is completely organic and is made of eggs, pepper and garlic. It is sprayed on the plants and will last up to 3 months depending on rain and growth rate of the plants.

HELP FROM THE DRAGON!

The Dragon's Eye Pine can be planted in direct sunlight and needs well-drained or clay soil and even tolerates high winds. Deer will not go anywhere near this pine. When planted in your garden, the early spring is the only time, this plant requires a little extra work, but expect excellent results.

OLD DOGGIE BLANKET WORKS GREAT

If you change your dog's blanket, don't throw it away if you have a deer or other small critter problem. Just cut up the blanket and leave pieces anywhere you have a problem with the critters.

PLANT SMELLY PLANTS

There are a number of plants that when planted in an area where deer frequent will deter them from munching on your trees and plants. These include rotunda Chinese holly, foxglove, Mexican oregano, mint, wormwood, spearmint, lemon thyme, Madagascar periwinkle and artemisias. Also planting thorny bushes such as blackberry or raspberry will act as a deterrent.

95% DEER-RESISTANT PLANTS

Ageratum	Daffodil	Myrtle
Ash	Daphne	Narcissus
Astilbe	Daylily	Nightshade
Black-eyed Susan	Devil's Poker	Oleander

Black Locust	Dogwood	Pampas Grass
Bleeding-heart	Dusty Miller	Peony
Blue Lily-of-the-Nile	English Ivy	Persimmon
Bottle Brush	English Lavender	Pine
Boxwood	Foxglove	Peppermint
Butterfly Bush	Giant Reed	Red Elderberry
Calla Lily	Hazelnut	Rosemary
Canterberry Bells	Holly	Scotch Broom
Carolina Cherry Laurel	Iceland Poppy	Solomon's Seal
Chives	Iris	Silvery Aremesia
Clematis	Japanese Rose	Spearmint
Columbine	Jasmine	Spruce
Coreopsis	Lamb's Ear	Tulip
Cransebill Gernaium	Larkspur	Yarrow

DEER & RABBIT RESISTANT PLANTS

Monkshood, anise hyssop, century plant, ornamental onion, showy blue-star, flame acanthus, mini mallow, dogbane, rock-cress, yellow prickly poppy, rose prickly poppy, white prickly poppy, jack-in-the-pulpit, horseradish, tarragon, white sage, silver mound, wild ginger, European ginger, pineleaf milkweed, desert milkweed, antelope horns, butterfly weed, green milkweed, astilbe, purple rock cress, basket of gold, false indigo, yellow datura, catus, bird of paradise, Windflower, mountain harebell, lindheimer senna,, two-leaved senna, tocalote thistle, Texas thistle, mountain pink, plumbago, night blooming jasmine, damianita, snakeroot, chicory, Threadleaf Coreopsis, Corydalis, Gregg Dalea, Datura, Jimsonweed, Queen Anne's Lace, Blue Larkspur, Fringed Bleeding Heart, Bleeding Heart, Snake Herb, Purple Coneflower,

NOT FOR BIRDS!

There is an organic repellant called Bird-X that is inexpensive and works great. It is made from a very high concentration of capsaicin and USP grade castor oil. This formula is active even after several watering's and a number of rains.

GIVE THEM THE SHOCK OF THEIR LIVES

Fences are usually not a good solution since deer can jump over most fences. An electrically charged fence, however, is a different story if built right. An electric fence only needs to be 5-feet high to be effective.

The fence needs to have 6 strands of wire with each strand starting at the bottom and is further away from the garden area than the one below it. This means that the fence must be at a 45^0 angle. When the deer sees the wire they will usually only see the top wire at the 5-foot level since the other wires are further away. When they try and go under the 5-foot wire they hit the lower wire and get the shock. Purchase the electric charger at any hardware store.

NOT AT ALL STICKY
If you plant molasses grass around your property it will repel deer and even trap their ticks in the sticky plant hairs.

CACKLEBERRY DETERRENT

4	Large raw eggs
1	Gallon of cool tap water

Place the eggs in the water and mix well, be sure that the water is not warm or the eggs will not mix well. Allow it to stand for 1 hour before straining and placing in a sprayer.

I TAUGHT I SAW A PUTTY TAT, SMELLED LIKE ONE!
This will keep deer far away from your property. If all else fails, go to your local zoo and ask them if you can have manure from the big cats cages.

I do mean the BIG cats including lions, tigers, leopards and panthers. This is guaranteed to keep deer away as long as the aroma lasts.

ATTACK OF THE CREEPING VINE
Deer will shy away from an area that has tomato and squash vines along the ground. If they are planted early before other plants so that they have some time to mature they will act as an excellent deer deterrent.

SPRINKLE SOME BLOOD
There are two excellent items that you can sprinkle around the areas to deter deer. They are blood meal or beef liver that has been processed. The blood meal can be purchased in any garden supply store. The raw liver (about ½ pound) needs to be placed in a food processor with 1 quart or less of water and then finely processed.

BUILD A MOAT

This is used quite a bit around small areas. Just place human hair in a shallow trench around the entire perimeter of the garden or trees you want to protect. This keeps the deer away and the birds have a ball using the hair for their nest. The hair is rich in nitrogen and can be worked into the soil after the deer season is over.

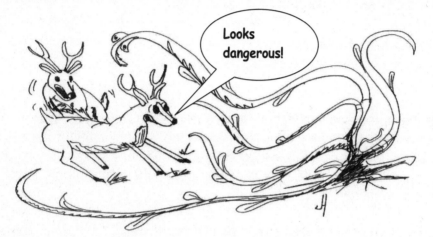

HIRE A DEAR, DEER DOG

Dogs are excellent deer deterrents. Deer will never come near a property that has a dog that is able to get to them.

NOT A PIPE DREAM

You can purchase thin plastic pipe and cut the pipe with a saw do that it will go around the trunk of the tree. This makes an excellent barrier not only for deer but other animals as well.

FORMULA 1 WITH EXCELLENT RESULTS

3 Raw eggs
3 Tbsp of red hot sauce
3 Tbsp of garlic juice or minced
Add enough water to a blender to process and mix well. Add this to a gallon of water and spray on plants.

FORMULA 2 WITH EXCELLENT RESULTS

2 Raw eggs
2 Cups cold water

Blend the 2 eggs and two cups or cold water at high speed then add this mixture to a gallon of water and allow it to stand for 24 hours. Spray on any foliage that deer frequent. The egg mixture does not wash off easily, but will need a re-application 2-3 times a season. For a larger quantity, blend a dozen eggs into 5 gallons of water. This mix will also repel rabbits.

FORMULA 3 WITH EXCELLENT RESULTS
6 Raw eggs
4 Hot peppers - make it very hot
6-12 Cloves of garlic - make it stink
5 Cups of warm water.

Put all the ingredients in a blender and liquefy then place it in a plastic container. Set it aside for a couple of days in the sunlight to let it cook and get really stinky and hot. Strain it good if you want to use it in a sprayer. The mixture can also be poured on and/or around the plants directly from the plastic container.

FORMULA 4 WITH EXCELLENT RESULTS
1 Raw egg
½ Cup low-fat milk
1 Tablespoon of cooking oil
1 Tablespoon of dish soap

Add 1 gallon of water and shake well. Spray or sprinkle on plants every two weeks or after heavy rain.

FORMULA 5 WITH EXCELLENT RESULTS
3 Large raw eggs, shells included
1 Large clove of garlic
2 Cups of fresh green onion tops
2 Cups of water

Place everything into a blender and liquify for about 2 minutes. Add the mixture to a pail containing 2 quarts of warm water and melted deodorant soap such as dial. Mix together then add two tablespoons of chili powder or cayenne pepper and mix well. Splash, spray, drip, or somehow paint the mixture on the plants.

Be sure and get egg shells on the leaves. When this formula is used every two weeks it is effective year-around. Best to save some of each batch to "ripen" the next batch!

FORMULA 6 WITH EXCELLENT RESULTS
1 Cup sour milk, sour cream, or buttermilk
2 Raw eggs beaten and strained
5 Drops of liquid dish soap
5 Drops of cooking oil or dormant oil
20 Drops of essential oil of cloves

Use a 1 gallon container with cold water. Shake well then spray as a light mist and you will have to re-spray every 2-3 weeks.

FORMULA 7 WITH EXCELLENT RESULTS
2 Tsp beef bouillon
2 Well-beaten raw eggs
1 Gallon of water

Dissolve bouillon and eggs in 1 gallon water. Let the mixture sit for a few days. Apply. Reapply after heavy rain.

FORMULA 8 WITH EXCELLENT RESULTS
Mix together in a blender:
2 Cups of water
5 Cloves of fresh garlic
1 Cup of chopped onions
5 Tbsp powdered hot pepper

Pour into a covered container and let stand for 24 hours. Strain and mix with 1 gallon of water then apply to plants with a sprayer.

FORMULA 9 WITH EXCELLENT RESULTS
4 Tbsp ground cayenne pepper
1 Cup white vinegar
½ Cup peeled garlic
1 Cup clear ammonia
1 Cup Murphy's oil soap
1 Bar Ivory hand soap or green mint soap (Optional)

Bring the cayenne and white vinegar to a boil for one minute then strain through a coffee filter. Puree the garlic in 2 cups of warm water then blend. Strain that mixture through another coffee filter then combine the two liquids with the ammonia and oil soap in a 3 gallon garden sprayer. Fill up the sprayer to the maximum level with water and spray on areas you wish to protect.

For extra stickiness, float bar of Irish Spring soap in the sprayer and use it over several fillings. Re-apply weekly especially after it rains.

CHAPTER 2

PETS

CATS & DOGS

CATS

GENERAL INFORMATION

The primitive ancestor of cats was a small, tree-living creature called a Miacis, which lived during the late Eocene period, some 45 to 50 million years ago. Phoenician cargo ships were thought to have carried the first domesticated cats to Europe in about 900 BC, however, the first true cats came into existence about 12 million years ago and were known as the Proailurus.

Ancient Egyptians were the first to tame the cat in about 3000 BC and used them to control rodents. Ancient Egyptian family members actually shaved their eyebrows in mourning when a family cat died. In Siam, the cat was so revered that they would ride in a chariot at the head of a parade when celebrating a new king.

The Pilgrims were the first to introduce cats to North America. The first breeding pair of Siamese cats arrived in England in 1884 and the first formal cat show was held in England in 1871, in America, in 1895.
The Maine Coon cat is America's only natural breed of domestic cat.

It is interesting that both humans and cats have identical regions in the brain responsible for emotion. A cat's brain is more similar to a man's brain than that of a dog. Cats also have a special scent organ that is located in the roof of their mouth, called the Jacobson's organ. This organ can analyze smells, and is the reason why you may sometimes see your cat "sneer," which is called the "flehmen" response, when they encounter a strong odor.

CAT FACTS

➤ A cat has more bones than a human; humans have 206, but the cat has 245, however, some bones may fuse together as the cat ages.
➤ Cats have 30 spinal vertebrae while humans have 33 vertebrae during early development then 26 after the sacral and coccygeal regions fuse.

- The cat's collarbone does not connect with the other bones and is deep in the muscles of their shoulder. The lack of a functioning collarbone allows the cat to fit through any opening the size of their head.
- The cat has 500 skeletal muscles while humans have 650.
- Cats must have fat in their diet because they can't produce it on their own.
- While many cats enjoy milk, it will give some cat's diarrhea.
- A cat will spend nearly 30% of her life grooming herself.
- When a domestic cat goes after mice, about 1 pounce in 3 results in a catch.
- Mature cats with no health problems are in deep sleep 15% of their lives. They are in light sleep 50 percent of the time. That leaves just 35% when they are awake or roughly 6-8 hours a day.
- Cats come back to full alertness from the sleep state faster than any other animal.
- A cat can jump 5 times as high as it is tall.
- Cats can jump up to 7 times their tail length.
- Cats have 32 muscles that control the outer ear compared to a human's 6 muscles for each ear. A cat can rotate its ears independently 180 degrees and can then turn in the direction of a sound at least 10 times faster than those of the best watchdog.
- Cats' hearing is actually much more sensitive than humans and dogs.
- A cat sees about 6 times better than a human at night. Cats have a layer of extra reflecting cells which absorb light.
- Studies have shown that cats can only see blue and green and possibly red.
- Unlike humans, cats do not need to blink their eyes very often to keep their eyes lubricated.
- It may take as long as 2 weeks for a kitten to acquire normal hearing. A kitten's eyes usually open between 7 and 10 days, but sometimes can happen earlier.
- Cats are able to judge within 3 inches the precise location of a sound being made 1 yard away.
- Cats can be right-pawed or left-pawed similar to a right or left-handed human.
- A cat is unable to see directly under its nose.
- Almost 10% of a cat's bones are found in its tail, which is used to maintain balance.

- The domestic cat is the only cat species that is able to hold its tail vertically while walking.
- Most cats love sardines.
- A cat uses its whiskers for measuring distances. The whiskers of a cat are capable of registering very small changes in air pressure.
- If a cat is frightened, its hair stands up fairly evenly all over the body. When cats are threatened or is ready to attack, the hair stands up only in a narrow band along the spine and tail.
- A cat has approximately 60 to 80 million olfactory cells (sense of smell) a human has between 5 and 20 million.
- Cats dislike citrus scent so use a citrus odor eliminator.
- A cat has a total of 24 whiskers, which amount to 4 rows of whiskers on each side. The upper two rows are able to move independently of the bottom two rows.
- When your cat rubs up against you, she is actually marking you as "hers" with her scent. If your cat pushes his face against your head, it is a sign of acceptance and affection.
- If your cat snores or rolls over on his back to expose his belly, it means he trusts you.
- Cats respond better to women than to men, probably due to the fact that women's voices have a higher pitch.
- Cats have 30 teeth (12 incisors, 10 premolars, 4 canines, and 4 molars), while dogs have 42. Humans usually have 20 primary (deciduous or "baby") teeth and 32 permanent, adult teeth.
- A cat's jaw only has up and down motion and does not have any lateral, side to side motion, similar to dogs and humans.
- A cat's tongue has very small barbs on it.
- Cats will lap liquid from the underside of their tongue, not from the top.
- Cats purr is at the same frequency as an idling diesel engine, about 26 cycles per second. Domestic cats purr both when inhaling and when exhaling.
- The cat's front paw has 5 toes, but the back paws have 4. Some cats are born with as many as 7 front toes and extra back toes and cats actually walk on their toes.
- A domestic cat can run at about 30 miles per hour.
- A kitten will usually weigh about 3 ounces at birth. The adult male housecat will weigh between 7 and 9 pounds, while the female weighs slightly less.
- The respiration rate for cats is between 20-40 breaths per minute.

- The normal body temperature for a cat is 102 degrees F compared to 98.6 for humans.
- A cat's normal pulse is 140-240 beats per minute, with an average of 195 compared to 72 for humans.
- Cat's urine will fluoresce (glows) under a black light.
- Cats can lose almost as much fluid in the saliva while grooming themselves as they do through urination.
- A cats two vocal chords can make over 100 sounds.
- There are approximately 100 breeds of domesticated cats.
- The life expectancy of cats has nearly doubled since 1930, from 8 to 16 years.
- Cats have been domesticated for half as long as dogs have been.

DIGGER THE CAT

The cat formula for keeping kitty out of the soft garden beds and using it as a latrine is a little different than for dogs. Mix together 2 tablespoons of cayenne pepper, 3 tablespoons of powdered Chinese mustard and 4 tablespoons of all-purpose flour in 2 quarts of warm tap water. Allow it to stand for 1 hour before straining and placing the mixture into a spray bottle. This will repel a mountain lion as well.

KEEP CATS AT BAY OR USE AS SALAD DRESSING

If you want to keep cats away from your property and especially the birdbath that Tweety Bird uses, just mix 2 ounces of white vinegar in a small sprayer bottle and give the area a squirt or two, but not in the bird bath water. Cats hate the smell of vinegar.

SCARE 'EM HALF TO DEATH

Cats are afraid of snakes! If you have a feline problem, just place an old piece of garden hose around your garden or get fake snake.

NOT VERY CATTY

Cats do not like to see their reflection in a plastic bottle. Try filling plastic soda bottles half full with water and leave them around the garden where they frequent. They will go looking for another area to use as a bathroom.

GET THE CATS WIRED

If you plant chicken wire just under the surface around the garden the cats have too much trouble digging and go find an easier area.

DRIVE THEM CRAZY

To keep cats away from your flowerbed or garden; just plant some catnip far away from the areas that you want to keep them away from. Cats will stay near the catnip plants. Be sure that the catnip plants are good healthy plants before you plant them so that they will have a good chance of surviving the cats.

THEY WILL "RUE" THE DAY

Cats do not like the herb "rue." If you scatter the rue leaves around the areas that they frequent they will leave very quickly. If you plant the herb near your garden that they are bothering they will not go there.

DOGS

GENERAL INFORMATION

Dogs can be traced back 40 million years to a weasel-like animal called the Miacis, which lived in trees and dens. The Miacis evolved into the Tomarctus, which is a direct decendent of the genus Canis, which includes the wolf and jackal as well as the dog. Ancient Egyptians revered their dogs and when a pet dog would die, the owners shaved off their eyebrows, smeared mud in their hair and mourned aloud for days.

The phrase "raining cats and dogs" originated in 17th century England. During heavy rainstorms, many homeless animals drowned and floated down the street giving the appearance that it had actually rained cats and dogs. During the Middle Ages, Great Danes and Mastiffs were occasionally suited with armor and spiked collars then enter a battle or defended supply caravans.

The oldest known identifiable dog bones were located in Asia and date as far back as 10,000 BC. The first identifiable dog breed appeared about 9000 BC, and was probably a type of Greyhound dog used for hunting.

DOG FACTS

➢ Small quantities of grapes or raisins can cause renal failure in dogs. Chocolate, macadamia nuts, cooked onions or anything with caffeine can also be harmful.
➢ Apple and pear seeds contain arsenic, which may be deadly to dogs.

- Dogs have sweat glands between their paws.
- In 2003, Dr. Roger Mugford invented the "wagometer," a device that claims to determine a dog's exact mood by measuring the wag of its tail.
- Dogs have three eyelids. The third lid is called a nictitating membrane or "haw" and keeps the eye lubricated and protected.
- A dog's shoulder blades are not attached to the rest of their skeleton, which allows greater flexibility for running.
- Puppies are sometimes rejected by their mother if they are born by cesarean section and cleaned up before being given back to her.
- Pekingese and Japanese Chins were so highly revered in ancient Far East that they had their own servants and were carried around trade routes as gifts for kings and emperors.
- The Mayans and Aztecs symbolized every tenth day with the dog, and those born under this sign were believed to have outstanding leadership skills.
- The first dogs were self-domesticated wolves, which at least 12,000 years ago, became attracted to the first sites of permanent human habitation.
- Dachshunds were bred to fight badgers in their dens.
- The term "dog days of summer" was coined by the ancient Greeks and Romans to describe the hottest days of summer, which coincided with the rising of the Dog Star, Sirius.
- A dog can locate the source of a sound in 1/600 of a second and can hear sounds at least four times farther away than a human can.
- Touch is the first sense the dog develops and the entire body, including the paws, is covered with touch-sensitive nerve endings.
- Eighteen muscles or more are required to move a dog's ear.
- There are an estimated 400 million dogs in the world.
- The U.S. has the highest dog population in the world. France has the second highest.
- Dog nose prints are known to be as unique as human fingerprints and can be used for identification.
- It is much easier for dogs to learn spoken commands, as long as they are given along with hand signals.
- Dogs can see in color, although they most likely see colors similar to a color-blind human. They can actually see better when the light is low.
- The average dog can run about 19 mph, however, greyhounds being the fastest dogs on Earth and can run at speeds up to 45 mph.

- Greyhounds are probably the most ancient dog breed. The word "Greyhound" comes from an error in translating from the early German name Greishund, which means "old (or ancient) dog," not from the color gray.
- The oldest dog on ever on record was an Australian sheep dog named Bluey who lived for 29 years. In human years, that is more than 160 years old.
- A person standing still at 300 yards away is almost invisible to a dog, however, a dog can identify its owner standing a mile away if the owner is waving his arms.
- Most dogs can smell 1,000 times better than humans. Humans have about 5 million smell-detecting cells and dogs have more than 220 million. The part of the dog's brain that interprets smell is also four times larger than in humans.
- Some dogs can smell dead bodies under water, where termites are hiding, opiates and natural gas buried under 40 feet of dirt. They can even detect cancer that is too small to be detected by a doctor and can find lung cancer by sniffing a person's breath.
- Dogs have a wet nose, which can collect more of the tiny droplets of smelling chemicals in the air.
- Dogs like sweets a lot more than cats do. Cats have around 473 taste buds; dogs have about 1,700 taste buds and humans have approximately 9,000.
- Dogs are about as smart as a 2-3 old child, meaning that they can understand about 150-200 words, including signals and hand movements with the same meaning as words.

THE DIGGING DOG

To stop dogs from digging your garden or flowerbed, just prepare a mixture of:

1	Finely chopped garlic clove
1	Really smelly onion chopped fine
1	Teaspoon of Tabasco Sauce™
1	Teaspoon of cayenne pepper

Place all the ingredients into 1 quart of warm tap water and allow it to stand overnight. Strain through a piece of cheesecloth or use a fine strainer and place the mixture into a spray bottle and spray around the areas. This should stop all critters, not just the dog.

REPELLENT SPRAY

2	**Cups of rubbing alcohol**
2	**Teaspoons of lemon grass oil**

Place the mixture into a sprayer and spray any areas that you would like the dog to stay away from.

KEEP THEIR LEGS ON THE GROUND

To eliminate your dog (male) urinating on a post or somewhere that they shouldn't, just grind up a few "cheap" cigars or several cigarettes and soak them in a bowl of tap water overnight. Spray or dribble the mixture in areas that you want them to avoid. *This is a toxic mixture and you don't want them to drink it.* Dispose of the leftovers safely and leave them someplace to go, so they don't run around with their legs crossed trying to find a spot to relieve themselves.

GOOD USE FOR THE OLD ROSE STEMS

When you trim the rose bushes in the fall save the stems with the prickly thorns on them and place them around the garden and the cats and dogs will not dig there. They will only try it once to get the idea.

BARRIER FOR NEIGHBORS DOGS

If you are having a serious problem with a neighbor's dog digging under your fence you can plant a prickly hedge or shrub such as Pyracantha. It is fast growing, looks nice and stops the problem.

HAVING A PROBLEM WITH YOUR CAN?

Dogs love to get into garbage cans! However, if you just sprinkle some ammonia around the base of the can they will steer clear.

DE-BURR-DEN YOUR PET

If your pet gets a burr in its coat, just apply a small amount of vegetable oil to the burr and allow it to remain for 5 minutes before combing it out. Sometimes if you crush the burr first with a pair of pliers it may hasten the removal.

CURING THE PAW-CHEWER

To cure a dog of paw, chewing, just paint the paw with oil of cloves. This will stop them from chewing instantly and wait until you see the look on their face.

DOES YOUR DOG LIKE TO PLAY TERMITE?

Puppies like to chew on wood, which can make the owner very unhappy if the wood is a good piece of furniture leg. Just paint the legs with oil of cloves to eliminate the problem.

SWEET SMELLING FLEA SHAMPOO FOR PETS

The following ingredients will be needed:

1	Cup Castile™ soap (liquid)
1/8	Ounce of essential oil of pine
1/8	Ounce of essential rose oil

Place all the ingredients into a jar with a lid and shake to mix well. Add the mixture to your pet's bath water and the fleas will be very unhappy.

ANIMAL DRY BATH FOR WINTER

The following ingredients will be needed:

1	Tablespoons of trisodiumphosphate (TSP)
2	Tablespoons of borax
4	Tablespoons of sodium carbonate
12	Tablespoons of talc
1½	Cups of starch

Place all the ingredients into a container and mix well. Rub the mixture on the animal against the direction of the hair; then brush well or vacuum to remove the dry shampoo.

If you would like to leave your pet sweet smelling, just add a few drops of your pets' favorite essential oil to the mixture.

OINTMENT FOR ANIMAL FLEA SORES
The following ingredients will be needed:

8	Ounces of lard
4	Ounces of beeswax
4	Ounces of rosin
½	Ounce of carbolic acid

Place the beeswax, lard and rosin in a double boiler and heat while stirring until melted, then add the carbolic acid and mix thoroughly. Remove from heat and allow the ointment to cool, then store in a well-sealed container until needed.

DO-IT-YOURSELF FLEA COLLAR
To rid your pet of fleas make your own all-natural flea collar, just cut a strip of cloth about an inch larger than the size of your pet's neck. Fold the cloth over with an opening in the center then sew one end shut as well as placing a seam down the strip. Using a funnel, fill the opening with a combination of 50/50 rosemary and oregano then sew or tape a piece of Velcro to close up the open end and attach it to the pet using a Velcro closure. Do not put pyrethrums in a cat collar but it can be used in a dog collar.

BASIC PET SHAMPOO
The following ingredients will be needed:

½	Cup of Castile™ soap (grated)

2½	Tablespoons of glycerin (from drug store)
3	Drops of pine oil or any scent your pet prefers
2	Tablespoons of denatured alcohol
1½	Cups of warm tap water

Place the soap and water in a double boiler and warm to melt the soap into the water, then add the glycerin and mix well. Remove the pan from the heat and allow the mixture to cool.

As it cools, add the alcohol and the pine drops, then mix well.

FLEA POWDER
Powder ½ cup of the following herbs and dust the animal. Use wormwood, fennel, rue and peppermint.

FIGHT FLEAS FROM THE INSIDE
A ratio of 1 teaspoon apple cider vinegar to 1 quart of water (per 40 pounds of pet weight) in their drinking water helps to keep your pets free of fleas and ticks.

MAKE SOME FLEA-ADE
Citrus oil is an excellent flea deterrent. Just slice up a lemon, score the skin to release more of the oil and then pour 1 cup of boiling water over the lemon and allow the lemon to sit overnight.

Use a clean sponge and sponge the lemon water on your pet to instantly kill the fleas. Best to give the pet a bath afterwards or they will smell like lemonade all day. If you buy a citrus product be sure it has D-limonene in it, since this will also kill ticks.

DO-IT-YOURSELF FLEA COLLAR
To make a flea collar, just soak a store-bought leather collar in the lemon juice (citrus oil) solution. You can also use a piece of cloth with a Velcro fastener. Most commercial flea collars use a pesticide, which are damaging to the environment.

GREEN BAN FROM DOWN UNDER
This shampoo is usually available from most pet stores or vets office. It is fresh smelling and contains pure essential oils that will eliminate the flea problem and leave your pet smelling spring fresh.

SCRUB-A-DUB-DUB

It is best to give your pet a bath regularly using just a mild soap or soap for pets from your pet store. When you brush your pet and find a flea soak the brush or comb in soapy water to kill the fleas. Also, if you add 1 teaspoon of white vinegar to 1 quart of water for every 40 pounds of body weight it will also help.

FLEA-ELIMINATOR FLOOR CLEANER

The following ingredients will be needed:

1	Tablespoon of liquid dish soap
4	Lemons (sliced thin)
5	Drops of pennyroyal (from health food store)
1	Gallon very warm water

Place the sliced lemons in a medium saucepan, cover with cold tap water and allow them to simmer on low heat for 1 hour. Remove the juice from the lemons and strain well. Place the juice into a bucket and add the soap, pennyroyal and water. Mix the solution very well before applying with a damp sponge mop. Allow the floor to dry before rinsing with a clean damp sponge mop.

ODE DE DOGGIE

To keep fleas out of your pets bedding, just sprinkle a few drops of lavender oil in their bed. Lavender oil can be purchased in most health food stores.

Spread leaves or shavings of the following plants under and around the pet's bed: Fennel, Rosemary, Red Cedar Shavings, Sassafras, Eucalyptus or Pennyroyal.

PET'S BEDDING FLEA ELIMINATOR
The following ingredients will be needed:

½	Cup of pennyroyal
2	Tablespoons of dried thyme
2	Tablespoons of dried wormweed
1	Tablespoons of dried rosemary

Place the herbs in a food processor and powder. Place the herbs inside your pet's pillow by opening up a seam, inserting the powder and sewing it back up making sure that the powder is as evenly distributed as possible.

FLEAS HATE SAGE
Fleas do not like the odor of sage. Crush up sage into a fine powder and rub it on your pet's skin, then allow it to remain for 15-20 minutes before brushing it off or vacuuming the pet if it is a big pet. **Vacuuming mini Chihuahuas is not recommended or they may be staring out from the clear plastic dirt tank.**

I hate vacuum cleaners

MAKING DOGGIE BISCUITS
The following ingredients will be needed:

¾	Cup of rye flour
1¾	Cups of whole wheat flour
¾	Cup of bulgur
½	Cup of cornmeal
½	Cup of Brewer's yeast (fresh from health food store)
1	Teaspoon of dry yeast
½	Cup of reduced fat dry milk
¼	Cup of warm tap water
1	Cup of de-fatted chicken or turkey broth

¼	Cup of dried parsley
1	Large egg (beat with 1 tablespoon of whole milk)

Place the warm water and dry yeast in a bowl and stir until all yeast is dissolved; then add the chicken or turkey broth. Place the flours, Brewer's yeast, bulgur, dry milk, cornmeal and parsley in another bowl and mix well. Stir the liquid mixture into the dry mixture and mix well into stiff dough. If the dough is too difficult to work, add a small amount of warm water to loosen it up.

Roll the dough out on a floured surface to about ¼ to ½ inch thickness, then cut with a cookie cutter into biscuits. Place the biscuits on a cookie sheet and lightly glaze with a beaten egg and bake at 300^0F for 40 minutes. Allow the biscuits to remain in the oven overnight to thoroughly dry out.

A SPOT OF TEA
A cup or two of cool peppermint tea added to your pets' bath water will also eliminate the fleas very effectively.

CALL FOR REINFORCEMENTS
Nc nematodes to the rescue! These beneficial worms will eliminate almost all of the flea larvae and pupae within 24 hours after the product is released. It is safe on vegetable gardens as well as lawns; however, it is best to spray the entire lawn area.

HERBS FOR YOUR PET
There are 3 herbs that you can feed to your pet to help keep fleas off; they are fennel, rue and rosemary.

DOG DEODORANT
The following ingredients will be needed:

1	Large size box of baking soda (fresh)
2	Pounds of cornstarch
2	Cups of dried pennyroyal
2	Cups of dried lavender
1¼	Cups of dried rosemary
2	Drops of essential lemon oil
15	Drops of citronella oil
2	Drops of essential rosemary oil
25	Drops of essential lemon oil
2	Drops of essential pennyroyal oil

Place the dried herbs in a blender and powder. Place all the ingredients into a small bucket, mix and allow it to stand in a cool, dark location for 2-3 days. Mix well and sprinkle where needed.

GETTING MISTY OVER FLEAS
Daily spraying of a fine mist prepared from Dr. Bronner's Peppermint Soap™ should do the trick; however, it needs to be done daily for the first week, then once a week for control for the next 4 weeks.

POWDER YOUR PET OR A NEIGHBOR WITH A PROBLEM
An excellent method getting rid of fleas on pets is to powder the pet with pure pyrethrum powder. It is safe for pets and people and works great. The animal should be powdered once or twice per week for the best results.

If you dust the bedding and carpet areas around the bed then vacuum it will help control the flea population. The pyrethrum powder should remain in place for about 1 hour before vacuuming any area that you powder.

PENNYROYAL BATH
Make a pot of pennyroyal tea and after it cools add it to the pet's bathwater to eliminate the fleas. Dried pennyroyal also works in the pets bedding to get rid of fleas.

COMB 'EM OUT, BUT DO IT OUTSIDE
A metal flea comb should be used if you have a serious flea problem. The comb will not only remove fleas but will get their eggs as well. If you do have a problem you should comb your pet twice a day for the best results.

WASH THEM FLEAS
Boil 1 quart of water, then add 1 cup of dried rosemary (fresh OK). Cover the pot and allow the mixture to steep until it is cool. Use to wash the pet, working it in and make sure you rinse the pet well.

THE FLEA HOTEL
Vacuuming is one of the most important things you can do to control the flea population on and around your pet. However, if you do not dispose of the vacuum bag or clean out the dust container after every vacuuming, it will turn into a flea hotel.

FLYING INSECT POTPOURRI
The following ingredients will be needed:

½	**Cup of pennyroyal**
1	**Cup of southernwood**
1½	**Cups of lavender flowers**
1½	**Cups rosemary**
½	**Cup of spearmint**
3	**Tablespoons of orris root**
½	**Cup of santolina**
¼	**Cup of tansy**
8	**Yellow tulips (dried well)**
¼	**Cup of mugwort**
¼	**Cup of cedarwood chips (fresh as possible)**

Place all the ingredients into a container and blend well, then place into a few potpourri baskets around the house. The aroma is pleasant except to flying insects.

HERE LITTLE FLEA
Check with your hardware store or garden supply house for a flea trap that uses a light bulb to attract them and a sticky base to capture them. These are very effective and inexpensive.

DON'T CROSS THE LINE
To keep your pets food safe from ants, just draw a line around the food dish with a piece of chalk. Ants will not cross the chalk line.

BUILD A FOOD DISH MOAT
If you place your pet's food dish in a shallow dish of soapy water so that it surrounds the food dish it will keep the ants out of the pet's food.

FLEA, CONTROL

The following ingredients will be needed:

1	**Pound of diatomaceous earth (from nursery, food grade)**
8	**Ounces of table salt**
2	**Ounces of peppermint powder**

Place the ingredients into a container that you will be able to sprinkle it out of. The container should have a sealed cap for shaking and mixing it and another cap with holes for sprinkling it out.

Shake the powder (try not to breathe in the mixture) on carpets where there may be a flea problem, then allow the powder to stand for 1 hour before thoroughly vacuuming it up. **Keep kids and pets off the carpet until it has been well vacuumed.**

A PILLOW FOR YOUR PET DOG
Most dogs like to rest their head on a pillow. To make a safe pillow that will not attract fleas, just place 2 ounces of pennyroyal, 1 ounce of thyme and 1 ounce of wormwood mixed together inside the pillow.

DOGGIE TREATS
The following ingredients will be needed:

1	**Cup of chicken**
1	**Cup of whole, wheat flour**
2	**Cups of standard oats**
2	**Large eggs**
1¼	**Tablespoon of garlic powder**
1	**Tablespoon of parsley**
2	**Tablespoons of soy sauce**
¼	**Cup of powdered whole milk**

Place the chicken in a medium saucepan and cook in chicken fat for 15 minutes then simmer for 35 minutes adding a small amount of water.

Remove from heat and allow the chicken to cool for about 20-30 minutes. Slice into small pieces and place all ingredients into a food processor and blend, but do not liquefy.

Place tablespoon size or larger globs on a cookie sheet and bake at 250^0F for 40-50 minutes, then allow to set-up in the sun (out of dogs reach) to fully dehydrate for a few hours. Allow the biscuits to cool for another 12 hours before allowing your pet to devour them.

A PILLOW FOR YOUR PET CAT
Cats will love this pillow contents and it will keep fleas away. Mix together 2 ounces of pennyroyal, 1 ounce of catnip and 1ounce of chamomile then place it inside of your cat's pillow.

POWDER FOR FLEAS

 The powder formula works on both cats and dogs and should be used whenever needed.

Mix together 2 ounces of pennyroyal, 1 ounce of wormwood, 1 ounce of rosemary and a dash or two of cayenne pepper. Try not to get the mixture in your pet's eyes.

THE CAT'S MEOW

Ingredients:

¾	Small can of tuna	½	Cup nonfat powdered milk
1	Tablespoon of corn oil	½	Cup whole-wheat flour
1	Large egg (beaten)	¼	Cup of water

Place the tuna in a large bowl and mash well. Add the flour and milk and mix together. Slowly stir in the water, egg and oil and mix well.

Shape into ½ to ¾ inch balls and place on greased baking pan.
Press the ball gently to flatten. Bake the tuna treats at 350^{0}F (175^{0}C) for 10 minutes then remove from oven. Allow the treats to stand for 5 minutes before tuning the treats over and baking for another 10 minutes.

Place the treats on a wire rack to cool then store in a well, sealed plastic container in the refrigerator.

SUPER-VITA MEAL FOR CATS

Ingredients:

5 Chicken livers (cooked in water & chopped)
2/3 Cup small curd cottage cheese
¼ Cup biscuit mix
2 Tablespoons corn or safflower oil
Pinch of salt

Mix all the ingredients together in a medium bowl and store in refrigerator and place into an airtight plastic container.

DUST THEM OFF

If you think your pet has fleas or ticks, just dust them with diatomaceous earth (DE, food grade) then allow it to remain for a few minutes before vacuuming the pet off.

SPRINKLING WITH DE

Just prepare a mixture of DE (food grade) and water and place the mixture in a watering can and spray the areas outside that the pet frequents the most. If you want a safer method, just use safe flea soap in water.

SWIMMING POOL FOR FLEAS

If you would like to catch the fleas, use a shallow pan half-filled with soapy water (use Ivory Liquid Soap™). Place a light over the pan to attract the fleas.

The fleas like the heat from the lamp and jump for the heat, fall into the water and lack swimming skills, so they drown. The soap eliminates the surface tension of the water and the fleas can't bounce out.

POP GOES THE FLEA

 Before this flea information was available grandpa used to catch the fleas and squeeze them until she heard a "pop." This is the oldest form of flea removal ever recorded.

However, this was not very practical since a flea can lay 1 egg per hour. This is by far the worst method ever used, since the flea may contain a disease and by crushing it, would release the disease.

MAKING EARWAX REMOVER FOR PETS

The following ingredients will be needed:

| ¼ | Cup of isopropyl alcohol |
| 10 | Drops of glycerin |

Place the ingredients into a small bottle and shake to mix well, then place a small amount (at room temperature) on a cotton swab and clean the pet's ears, very gently. The pet will probably shake their head, which will help clean out the wax. Be careful to remove the swab if the pet shakes their head to avoid damage to the eardrum.

THE ORANGE RUBDOWN

Just score the peel of an orange and rub the peel on the animal's skin. This will repel fleas on most animals. You can also use the peels from 3-4 oranges or lemons and place them into a blender then rubdown the pet with the solution using a sponge. You might want to give them a bath 30 minutes after and keep them outside until the bath time.

DOGGIE BAGELS

Ingredients:
2   Cups of whole-wheat flour
2/3   Cup of beef broth
1   Large egg
1   Teaspoon of garlic powder
3½   Tablespoons of quick oats

Blend the broth and egg together in a large bowl then add the blend to the flour. Blend in the oats and garlic powder to form the dough into a ball. Using a floured work surface; roll the dough into about ½ inch thick pieces. Shape into bagels making the hole with your thumb and arrange on a shallow baking pan allowing space between each bagel.

Microwave the bagels on high setting for about 10 minutes then allow them to cool on a wire rack before refrigerating.

THE FLANNEL TRAP

Place a piece of flannel in your dogs bed and let him lay there for a few minutes then get him up and check the flannel for fleas. This is a good test to see how bad the infestation really is. Wash the flannel immediately in hot water.

SOCK IT TO THEM

If you walk around the house with a pair of athletic socks they will pick up fleas. Just check the socks for fleas and throw them into the washer immediately.

ANTI-TICK GROUND COVER

There are a number of ground covers that seem to repel ticks or at least discourage them from staying around very long. They are molasses grass, sage, pyrethrum and lavender. Studies have shown that there are fewer ticks in areas where these ground covers grow.

PARASITES

WORMS IN DOGS & CATS

There are several worm parasite that your pet can become the victim of, such as roundworms, whipworms, hookworms and tapeworms to mention a few of the more common ones. They can be detected in the animal's stool. These parasites are capable of causing diarrhea, weight loss, dry hair, poor appearance and vomiting (which may contain worms).

Some worm eggs, however, can remain dormant and cause no symptoms at all. Some worm larvae can actually be dormant until the animal is under stress. If the problem is not taken care of, the worms can even infest new born puppies or kittens.

Roundworm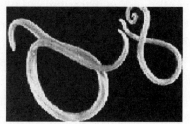

NATURAL REMEDIES FOR WORMS

The most common parasite problem in companion animals are intestinal worms (roundworm, tapeworm, hookworm and whipworm) and heartworm. There are two natural remedies for expelling worms: Only Natural Pet Para-Gone™, which is an herbal complex and Homeo-Pet Worm Clear™, which is homeopathic combination remedy.

Both remedies require regular dosing 3 times per day for 10 to 14 days. We do not recommend giving both remedies at the same time, but you can give one and then follow with the other if need be. It can take up to 3 days or more for the worms to begin to be eliminated, depending on the overall health of the animal and whether or not the animal is constipated.

The worms will easily pass out of the animal's system in their stools. If the animal is constipated, a laxative herb is recommended.

PREVENTION IS BEST

If you add some powdered pumpkin seeds and a small amount of garlic to your pet's diet they will probably never get worms and if they do, the worms will probably pack up and leave.

HEARTWORM IN YOUR PET

Heartworms are transmitted by mosquitoes, which are present almost year-round in some areas of the country. While there have been very few cases of West Nile Virus reported in canines, it's still wise to observe the following precautions suggested by the ASPCA Animal Poison Control Center (APCC). These tips can help safeguard human family members as well.

> - Keep pets indoors at dawn, dusk and early evening when mosquitoes are most active.
> - Eliminate areas of standing water that can serve as breeding grounds for mosquitoes, and remember to recheck your pet after each rainfall.
> - Change any outdoor water bowls a couple times a day to prevent mosquitoes from using them to lay their eggs.
> - The APCC does not recommend the use of mosquito control products that contain DEET™. Dogs and cats are extremely sensitive to DEET and may develop neurological problems if a product formulated with DEET is applied to them.

- Some topical flea and tick control products for dogs such as Frontline™ and K9 Advantix™ contain mosquito repellent.
- Avoid using pest control products with concentrated essential oils such as tea tree, pennyroyal and d-limonine. These concentrates have caused weakness, paralysis, liver problems and seizures in pets, plus their effectiveness is not proven.

TICKS & FLEAS

General Information:

Ticks are related to spiders and can harbor a number of different diseases. There are hard ticks and soft ticks. The hard tick can produce up to 10,000 eggs after one feeding. Soft ticks can feed several times and lay 30-50 eggs after each feeding. If you feel that you have been bite by a tick, it would be best to see your doctor as soon as possible. Ticks take their time when feeding since they do not fall off easily they are in no rush and can enjoy their meal. They are actually more dangerous than fleas and mosquitoes.

There are over 800 species of ticks in the United States and they will feed on animals, birds and humans. They wait on a tall piece of grass until a suitable host passes by and then jumps or flies on them.

A tick will not bite a human immediately and will search for the best spot. It has a curved set of teeth that hang on then secretes a cement-like substance, which helps it stick on to its host. Ticks can feed for several days on a host if not found.

Prevention and Control of Ticks, Around the Home:

- Make sure the property around your home is unattractive to ticks. Because ticks are sensitive to dry conditions and do not thrive in short vegetation, they are seldom a problem in well-maintained lawns. Keep your grass mowed and keep weeds cut.
- Clean up items that attract rodents which can carry ticks, such as spilled birdseed, and hiding places like old wood piles.
- If ticks are present in vegetation along the edge of the property, natural insecticides labeled for control of ticks can be applied to small areas of high weeds that cannot be mowed.

Often, one or two applications per season will be adequate to control ticks in these areas.

➢ Free-roaming dogs and cats are much more likely to encounter ticks than those that are confined to the home or yard. If ticks are found on pets, contact your veterinarian for information about an appropriate tick treatment.

➢ Remove the occasional tick found indoors by vacuuming, seal the vacuum bag and place it in the trash. When to Contact a Physician after a Tick Bite

➢ If you experience a rash that looks like a bull's-eye, or a rash anywhere on the body or an unexplained illness accompanied by fever following a tick bite, you should consult your physician and explain that you were bitten by a tick. Disease carried by ticks can be treated with antibiotics. However, the type of antibiotic can vary and individuals should be treated early in the infection.

MY DOG HAS CAT FLEAS

Fleas are usually brought into your home by your pet or visitor's pet. If you find one flea there is probably 100 more for every one you find somewhere in your pets environment. Fleas can jump 150-200 times their body length and one pair of fleas can produce 250,000 more fleas or up to 1 trillion in a year. They are like little vampires and like warm-blooded hosts.

The most common flea is the **"cat flea,"** which can be found on your dog. It would be best to treat areas that fleas may frequent before you have a problem, because afterwards it is really hard to get rid of them. The flea cycle is as follows: the flea jumps on your pet and has a warm blood meal. If your pet is not available, you are next. Once they have fed, they will mate and lay eggs (and are not fussy where they lay them).

48

It will take 2-3 weeks to hatch the hundreds of eggs, which release small caterpillar-like (larvae) creatures, which feed on almost any organic matter they find. After it has fed, it spins a cocoon (pupae stage). When the flea is in the pupae stage it cannot be killed in the cocoon. No chemical spray will penetrate the cocoon. When it hatches, you have more fleas. Treating your yard is one of the best methods of controlling a flea population. Professional help is usually needed if you have a bad infestation.

One of the most common reasons pets get fleas is that they have dry, flaky skin, which makes it easier for the fleas to get a foothold and is easier for them to obtain their meal of blood. If the animal gets adequate exercise they will not have as many fleas.

Fleas and ticks cause a number of problems in pets. Fleas feed on animal blood and can trigger problems including skin irritation, allergic reactions, anemia, and in rare cases even death. They can also carry tapeworms, which can infest your pet. If you see small rice-like particles around the dog's anus or in his feces, he probably has tapeworms. Ticks also carry diseases such as Lyme, ehrlichiosis, babesiosis and Rocky Mountain Spotted Fever, so you don't want them feeding on your pet.

FLEA PREVENTION
 ➤ Chemical and drug-free methods to keep your pet from getting "bugged" include inspecting your pet each day, and better yet, after each outing outdoors and don't forget to use the lint roller!

- Use a flea comb to search for and remove fleas. Use tweezers or a tick scoop to remove any other bugs and burrs.
- You can dab some petroleum jelly on the comb to help make the fleas stick to its tines.
- Gather a cotton ball, alcohol and cup filled halfway with warm soapy water. Soak the cotton ball in alcohol before combing.
- Remember to check between your dog's toes, behind and in the ears, in the armpits and around the tail and head.
- Comb your pet over white paper. If fleas are present, you will see tiny black specks fall on the paper.
- To check your dog for fleas when bathing, place a large white towel beneath your dog. Fleas typically fall off when you rinse the dog, so you're likely to spot them on the towel.
- Trix™ no-touch tick remover is reportedly safe and effective for even sensitive areas such as the ears.

IF YOU FIND A FLEA – WHAT TO DO!

- Dab the fleas with a cotton ball soaked in alcohol. This slows down fleas, enabling you to catch them. Then plunge the fleas to the bottom of the cup of water. Next, dump the water into the toilet and flush, or rinse down a sink, to prevent the flea from escaping.
- Smother fleas by dropping them in a cup of water to which a teaspoon of cooking oil has been added.
- When finding a tick a tick, carefully remove the whole tick from the pet's body. A tick scoop, available at many pet supply stores, is best for removing ticks.
- See www.tickedoff.com for tick scoop details.
- How to remove a tick using tweezers: Grasp the tick as close to the skin as possible by gripping its head. Steadily and slowly, pull upward until the tick releases his grip.
- Never twist or jerk a tick or you might break off the head or mouth parts, and you do not want to leave the tick head embedded in your pet's skin, which may cause infection.
- Never squeeze to the point of crushing the tick, or disease-spreading secretions may be released. If you do not have tweezers or a tick scoop, you can use your fingers, a loop of thread around the jaws, or a needle between the jaws to pull it out.

- If the head is left in the skin, use a sterile needle to remove the head similar to how you would remove a splinter. Wash the tick bite and your hands with soap and water, and apply antibiotic ointment to the bite.
- Studies show that using petroleum jelly, alcohol and hot match heads do not work to loosen ticks from skin, although a few people still use the petroleum jelly and rubbing alcohol approaches, but the hot match technique has caused skin injuries.
- Another way to remove a tick is to apply liquid soap to a cotton ball. Cover the tick with the soap-soaked cotton ball and swab it for 15 seconds. We're told the tick will release and come out when you lift the cotton ball.
- Ticks do not drown in water, so dispose of them by wrapping in a tissue and flushing down the toilet, or drowning in rubbing alcohol. Do not crush the tick since that can spread disease. Some vets may want to see the tick if disease transmission is suspected.
- Swab the pet's bitten area with antiseptic.

NATURAL METHODS OF PREVENTION & TREATMENT

Remember, fleas and other parasites have less effect on healthy animals and they tend to live on pets that are unhealthy and have weak immune systems. Healthy animals recover from illness faster and in the case of contracting parasites are less likely to get sick. It's a matter of immunity!

You also need to be aware that stressful conditions, such as parasites weaken immunity in both humans and animals. Chemical-free, drug-free ways to keep your pet from getting "bugged" include inspecting your pet each day, and better yet, after each outing outdoors.

A growing number of pet owners use natural ingredient-based flea repellents, immunity-boosting dietary measures and other techniques, instead of chemicals and commercial medications. Following are some natural, holistic approaches that many people find effective.

BOOSTING PETS IMMUNITY & REPELLING BUGS
- A half teaspoon of Brewer's yeast daily can provide the B complex vitamins a dog needs.

- Make sure it is Brewer's yeast or nutritional yeast (but not baker's yeast), and give 1 teaspoon per 30 pounds of body weight mixed with the animal's food.
- B complex vitamins - 50 mg once a day for cats and smaller dogs and twice daily for larger dogs.
- Use Omega 3 and 6 fatty acid supplements.
- Add a tablespoon of organic apple cider vinegar to the dog's water bowl as a blood cleanser.
- Add .a teaspoon each of safflower oil and powdered kelp or seaweed to the food bowl.
- Fresh garlic in small quantities can help repel fleas by making the animal taste unpleasant to fleas. Just grate a small amount of fresh, raw garlic into your pet's food at mealtime, about one-half to 3 chambers of the clove (chamber, not a whole clove) depending on the animal's size.
- Some vets recommends one crushed clove of garlic (not a whole bulb; a clove is just one chamber) per every 30 pounds.
- In fact, some holistic health practitioners recommend heating the garlic for easier digestion, and to not to give them garlic every day, but 4times a week.

ALL-NATURAL SPRAYS, LOTIONS & SHAMPOOS
- Several useful, relatively gentle flea shampoos to help rid fleas. Avoid shampoos with insecticides, since the chemicals can be harsh. If your dog has fleas, use a gentle shampoo containing pyrethrin, pyrethrum or citrus oil.
- When bathing your pet, you can use apple cider vinegar to rinse his or her fur. Fleas don't like the smell or taste.
- Lavender, peppermint and geranium essential oils repel mosquitoes. Lavender, lemongrass and geranium repel ticks. Also, lavender, lemongrass, peppermint and citronella repel fleas.
- Dab oils between the dog's shoulder blades. Lavender (which also repels flies) is particularly versatile.
- Other effective natural repellents include lemon, cedar, eucalyptus, myrrh and rosewood.
- Put a drop of lemon oil or rosemary oil on the dog's collar.
- A safe, easy homemade flea repellent: cut 6 lemons in half, boil in a quart of water, steep a few hours, then strain the solution into a spray bottle. Mist your pet's fur, taking care not to spray near the eyes.

Don't spray anything in a dog's face; apply spray to the hand and then rub it on the fur.

➢ Another gentle homemade flea spray: dilute a flower-scented shampoo, such as the type available from ihelppets.com, in water and spray liberally, or rub into the coat and let air-dry.

➢ One inexpensive over-the-counter choice for dogs and cats is Gentle Touch™ drops. Gentle Touch™ is all-natural and free of chemicals and petroleum solvents.

➢ Bothered by flies? Pyrethrin-based sprays and ointments are relatively safe and effective.

➢ You can find many natural products for flea and tick control on the internet, including: www.preciouspets.org/fleafree.htm and www.greenpet.com.au/article_fleas.php.

➢ Animal Essentials™, Green Hope Essences™ and Vetriscience™ are among many companies that make products designed to boost the immune system and help heal the skin.

➢ Quantum's 100% Natural Herbal Skin Conditioning Spray™ repels ticks and fleas. Ingredients include essential oils such as rose geranium, eucalyptus and tree tea, extracts of St. John's Wort, Rue, wormwood, basil and black walnut hulls.

➢ A single female flea can produce up to 50 eggs a day, Comfortis® (spinosad) for dogs starts killing fleas before they lay eggs and provides a full month of flea protection to help prevent flea infestations.

➢ In fact, veterinarians give Comfortis® the highest overall satisfaction rating when compared to other monthly flea control products and Comfortis® is easy to administer. It is a beef-flavored, chewable tablet that can be offered as a treat.

➢ Comfortis® flea protection is available through veterinarians, so you can feel confident you're getting the right dosage for your dog. Ask your veterinarian if Comfortis® is right for your dog.

TICKS THAT CAUSE DISEASE

American dog tick

One of the most common ticks is the American dog tick, also sometimes known as the wood tick. The larvae and nymphs feed on small warm-blooded animals such as rats, mice and birds.

However, the adult American dog tick will feed on humans and medium to large mammals such as raccoons and dogs.

Before feeding males and females are, reddish-brown and about 3/16-inch long. Females have a large silver-colored spot behind the head and will become ½-inch long after feeding or about the size of a small peanut. Males have fine silver lines on the back and do not get much larger after they have fed. Male ticks are sometimes mistaken for other species of ticks because they appear so different from the female.

The American dog tick can transmit Rocky Mountain spotted fever and tularemia to humans.

BASIL WILL WORK
Crush the entire basil plant and place the basil into 2 quarts of water. Allow it to remain for 2 hours before straining and using in a sprayer. Fresh basil has been used to control ticks for hundreds of years.

USE A LINT ROLLER
Lint rollers that you can usually purchase at your dry cleaners are a roller with sticky tape on them used to pick up lint. These can be used very efficiently to roll over a dog or cat and pick up fleas and ticks.

A CHILLY SOLUTION
Ticks are attracted by carbon dioxide, which is expelled by all animals. Ticks can be trapped using the dry ice method. You can make a dry ice trap by following the directions:

You will need a covered bucket approximately 6X6X12. Any type of container will do as long as it is about the right dimensions.
Drill or cut four ¾ inch holes near the bottom of the container spaced evenly. This will allow the dry ice vapor to be released and attract the ticks.

Drop about 2 pounds of dry ice into the container, which will last about 3 hours before it will dissipate. It will capture all ticks in about a 75-100 square foot area during the 3-hour period.

Place the container on top of a piece of plywood and place masking tape sticky-side up on top of the plywood. Attach the tape with staples and remove the masking tape and replace it as the ticks are trapped

TICK REPELLANT
Crush up the following herbs and place the mixture into a small muslin bag, then leave the bag near the pets bedding. Use about ½ ounce of each.

Dried peppermint, eucalyptus, bay leaf, sage, rosemary, cloves and marjoram.

FLEA AND TICK COLLARS
Use a pyrethrum-based flea collar for best results. *DO NOT USE A PYRETHRUM COLLAR ON A CAT.* Cats are allergic to pyrethrum and may break out in a rash.

TICKS HATE GARLIC
Finely chop 5 cloves of garlic and allow them to soak in 4 teaspoons of water for 24 hours. Strain the mixture and use 1 part per 20 parts of water then place in sprayer. This will kill a number of insects as well as the ticks and fleas. Make sure that you only use garlic in glass containers since garlic may react with metal.

GIVE THEM A GREASE JOB
To get a tick off your pet, just rub a small amount of oil on the tick. This tends to suffocate the tick and they withdraw almost immediately. This will stop the tick from injecting its poisons and is the recommended method of removing them safely.

PET NUTRITIONAL TIPS
There are certain essential nutrients that poets should have and many pet owners are not aware of. The following is a few of these key nutrients:

OMEGA FATTY ACIDS
Omega 3, 6 and 9 fatty acids are essential for dogs and cats. Their bodies cannot make these essential fatty acids, so they need to be obtained in the diet. It's best if the omegas are consumed in their natural ratio but the typical pet' diet is unbalanced, with a poor ratio.

Pet food is manufactured mainly from leftovers of human food processing, dogs and cats receive plenty of Omega-6's (from vegetable oils and animal fats) through their food, but very little of the Omega-3 fatty acids. Two of the essential fatty acids EPA and DHA are the most important Omega-3s for pets. EPA is an important fatty acid and an important element of every cell membrane having powerful anti-inflammatory properties.

DHA, another fatty acid helps develop and keep the eyes and brain healthy. By incorporating these essential fatty acids into the pet's diet you may reduce inflammatory processes in the body, thus lessening the effects of arthritis and other associated joint problems related to inflammation.

The best sources of Omega-3 fatty acids for pets are oils, such as fish oil and cod liver oil, which can be assimilated immediately by the body.

DIGESTIVE ENZYMES

Digestive enzymes are normally produced by the body and are active in breaking down foods so they can be absorbed and used by the body. If food is not broken down efficiently, some of those indigested particles may set off an immune response that can result in inflammation, allergies, and other health problems.

Digestive enzymes are of particular concern in older pets since the pancreas, which is responsible for producing most of the digestive enzymes loses efficiency as the pet grows older. Raw foods contain enzymes as long as they are not cooked, since cooking destroys the enzymes. If you purchase a supplement, be sure that it contains protease, amylase, lipase, and cellulase.

ANTIOXIDANTS

Antioxidants scavenge and neutralize an abnormal cell produced by the body called a "free radical." There is a school of thought that relates free radicals to the origination of cancer cells. While people usually acquire enough natural antioxidants from a diet high in fresh fruits, grains and vegetables, pets are eating processed pet food, which is lacking in sufficient antioxidants and typically too high in Omega-6 fatty acids that promote inflammation, so supplementing with antioxidants is very important. Since antioxidants work synergistically together, be sure and choose a product that has a combination of several good antioxidants in it, such as Vitamin E & C and carotenoids.

HORSES

General Information

TAKING CARE OF A HORSE

Grooming Tips
  ➤ Best to body clip your horse in the winter and it will make grooming and cooling out much easier.
  ➤ If the weather is warm enough, give your horse a soap bath before you clip him then do a final rinse with a fabric softener solution.

This will help make the clippers glide through his coat and reduce the number of tramlines.

➢ If it is too cold outside to bath your horse, a thorough grooming is a good idea. Dirt dulls the blades and leaves the coat looking rough.

➢ When you have finished clipping, dip a rag in either warm water and baby oil or warm water and alcohol, ring it out well and go over the entire horse to remove loose hair and scurf and leave your horse smooth and shiny.

➢ Be sure to keep a clipped horse warm and dry.

➢ When you give your horse a soap bath, try rinsing with white vinegar will help to remove the soap. White vinegar will also act as a natural hair conditioner and even a fly repellant.

➢ Place half a cup of pine cleaner and half a cup of fabric softener in a small bucket of hot water then wring out a rub rag in this mixture and use it to remove dust, dirt and germs from their coat. This solution will also soften the coat and leave a great shine.

➢ To untangle a matted tail, try washing it with soap and water. Ivory liquid will work well then rinse and apply a hair conditioner following the instructions on the bottle. Allow the tail to dry and then carefully untangle the mat. A plastic comb with large teeth will work well. You will probably loosen some tail hair as the tangle comes out.

➢ For a really bad tangle, repeat the process a couple of times.

Health Care

➢ When winter arrives and the weather gets cold you need to pay extra attention to your horse. Make sure your horse is drinking plenty of water.

➢ When the temperature drops horses often stop drinking which can lead to colic.

➢ Provide a mineral block for your horse and add salt to his feed to encourage him to drink plenty of water. Also try offering luke warm water. This does not shock the stomach like ice cold water and many horses appreciate having the chill taken off.

➢ Spring is the time for booster shots, which include flu, tetanus, Eastern and Western Encephalitis and Rhino. Depending on where you live your horse may also need rabies, Potomac fever and other regional vaccinations. Check with your Vet for the appropriate vaccinations for your area.

- During wet weather, carefully check your horse heels for signs of scratches or cracked heels. Wash these wounds with iodine shampoo and dry with a towel. Using Desitin on these wounds helps them to heal and prevents new sores.
- Be sure your horse is on a regular deworming schedule? If not, you need to start one if the weather is cold and unpredictable, your horse needs to be carefully monitored so that he maintains his condition. A good deworming program will help your horse get the most from his food.
- Be sure and keep a container of Gold Bond powder in your barn. Gold Bond can be used to treat rain rot and thrush. It is also useful in preventing rubs from protective boots.
- Appling Vaseline around horse's eyes will repel flies. Also applying lard to horses face keeps the flies away.
- A good treatment for severe or chronic thrush is to flush the affected area thoroughly with water then use hydrogen peroxide to kill all the anaerobic bacteria. Dead tissue should be removed by your farrier or vet.
- To promote new growth and healing use Sugardine. Sugardine is made of equal parts Betadine scrub and table sugar. Mix the two until you have a paste and if possible pack with cotton soaked in Sugardine and bandage.
- The Betadine fights bacteria and the sugar provides the correct PH balance for new tissue growth. Sugardine works on most wounds as well. It is especially good for sole abscesses.

Stable Management
- To make a broom last longer, be sure and turn it 180^0 frequently as you sweep. This will help keep the broom even and as the broom wears down, tidy up any ragged ends with scissors and remove the top two restraining strings from around the bristles.
- If cobwebs are driving you crazy, once you have them knocked down, wash the walls with a Lysol solution. The mixture does not need to be very strong to discourage spiders and repel flies. One washing should last you all summer.
- When purchasing blankets for your horse, be sure they fit properly. Measure your horse from the center of his chest going around his side to a point in the center of his tail. This will be the size in inches that he needs.

Be sure that blankets do not press on the withers and cause sores. A well, fitting blanket has no pressure points and will remain in place when the horse lies down or rolls.

➤ If your horse tends to loose, the hair on his shoulders spray them with show sheen before putting on his clothes. Blanket liners also help prevent these unsightly bald spots.

Tack Tips

➤ In order to find a saddle that will fit your horse, it is helpful to make a wire template. To make a template of your horse's withers use flexible wire, such as floral decorating wire. Bend the wire across the horse's withers at the point at which the pommel would normally rest. (To find this point place a saddle on your horse and make a note of where the pommel sits.) Bend the wire downward on both sides, molding it against the horse's shoulders; it should be in contact with the horse on both sides and on the withers.

➤ You need to have at least eight inches of wire on each side extending downward from the withers to the shoulders. Once you have made your outline of the withers with wire, trace it onto a piece of 8 1/2 by 11-inch paper. Cut away the excess paper so that only the shape of the withers and shoulders remains.

➤ Take this template with you when you are looking for a new saddle. By holding the template underneath the pommel of a saddle it is possible to see how the saddle will fit your horse.

➤ A well, fitting saddle does not press on the withers nor does it pinch the shoulders. To test this you should be able to slide two fingers between the saddle and the withers.

➤ A wet chamois will help prevent your saddle from slipping. Wring out the chamois and place it under the saddle pads, directly on the horses back.

Making Your Life Easier

➤ In winter smear Vaseline in water buckets before filling them with water. This will make the ice much easier to remove. It should just slide out when the bucket is tipped up!

➤ Before riding in snow, smear a layer of Vaseline on the inside of your horse's hoof. This will prevent ice and snow from balling up inside the hoof. If you don't have Vaseline handy then spray a thin layer of cooking spray on the bottom of the hoof.

➢ Try using duct tape when your horse pulls a shoe. Applying strips of tape to a barefoot will help to prevent the hoof wall from cracking and breaking away. To make a more substantial pad, wrap a rag around the hoof before applying the duct tape. Diapers are also great for temporary hoof protection. Again, secure the diaper with duct tape.

SPECIAL TIP

This tip is for young horse lovers who may be intimidated by horses or even afraid of the animals they love. Try spending a lot of time with horses. Talking to your horse will help build friendship and trust. Give commands with a strong tone of voice. Spend time with your horse observing his natural moves and reactions from the ground. Take a walk with your horse and see the world as he sees it, begin to learn how he reacts to the world. Gaining your horse's trust and confidence and letting him know that you are in control will help with your confidence level.

CHAPTER 3

RODENTS

MICE

General Information:

  Mice, while looking cute can cause damage to electrical wiring, clothing and food stores. The U.S. Environmental Protection Agency estimates that one pair of mice in a six month period can consume about four pounds of foodstuffs and contaminate another 40 pounds while leaving 20,000 droppings along the way. A pair of mice can produce up to 50 young in a one-year period. Trapping them is still one of the best methods.

HOUSE MOUSE
The house mouse is the most common rodent in the world. Their diet usually consists of plants, but they will also eat insects, meat and dairy products. They drink water but require very little of it. Also, they will eat their own droppings to acquire nutrients produced by bacteria in their guts!

House mice always live in structures, but they can live outdoors. They will breed throughout the year and often share nests with their "relatives".

House mice will eat 15-20 times a day, so keep your homes clean and do not leave food out. Be sure to empty kitchen and household garbage cans frequently and make sure that your home and storage areas are clean and dry since they prefer some moisture.

The smallest amount of mouse urine can trigger allergies in susceptible individuals, particularly in children since their immune systems are still developing. Mice tend to spread disease through bite wounds and by contaminating food and water with their waste materials.

Mice can also spread disease by harboring ticks, fleas and mites. These parasites will bite and infect the mouse then spread the disease by biting humans.

DEER MICE

Deer mice prefer to eat seeds, small fruit and berries, but will also eat beetles, caterpillars, grasshoppers, leafhoppers, and some species of underground fungus. Their favorite diet is insects when they can easily find them.

They make their home outdoors in hollow tree logs or piles of garbage. Since they are nocturnal they sleep in their nests during the day and use their nests to raise their young and to provide protection against harsh weather. When they do come indoors, they prefer quiet places, such as attics where it is also warm.

Deer mice are capable of spreading the potentially fatal Hantavirus, which can be spread by touching infected mice or by breathing in the fumes released in their urine.

Deer mice eat 15-20 times a day, so keep your homes clean and do not leave food out. Be sure and empty kitchen and household garbage cans frequently. Be sure that your home and storage areas are clean and dry and that you clean your sheds and garbage cans often.

Best to close up any small holes and cracks they can come in through.

TRAPPING MICE & RATS

Trapping is an effective method of controlling mice, but requires more work than most other methods. It is recommended where poisons seem inadvisable such as in a home where children and pets are present. It is the preferred method to try first in homes and other small structures where there may be only a few mice present.

Trapping has a number of advantages: (1) it does not rely on dangerous rodenticides; (2) it allows the user to see their success; and (3) it allows for easy and safe disposal of the mice, eliminating odor problems from decomposing carcasses that may remain when poisoning is done within buildings especially in attics.

The best trap is the simple, inexpensive, wood-based snap trap, which is available in most hardware and farm supply stores. Traps need to be baited with a small piece of nutmeat, chocolate candy, dried fruit, bacon or peanut butter securely attached to the trigger. Peanut butter or marshmallows seem to be the preferred bait. Since mice are always in search of nesting materials, sometimes a small cotton ball will also work as bait when attached securely to the trigger. When food baits become stale they lose their effectiveness.

Traps should be set close to walls, behind objects, in dark places and especially in locations where mouse activity has been seen. Place the traps so that when mice follow their normal course of travel (usually close to a wall) they will pass directly over the trigger. Be sure and set traps so that the trigger is very sensitive and will spring easily. Effectiveness can be increased by making the trigger larger.

Best to use enough traps to make the event short and decisive! Mice seldom venture far from their safe shelter and food supply, so traps need to be spaced no more than about 6 feet apart in areas where mice are active. Mice are not nearly as afraid of new objects as rats are so try leaving the traps baited but unset until the bait is taken at least once or twice since this will reduce the chance of mice escaping the trap and becoming trap-shy.

MOUSE TRAPS
There are a number of multiple-capture, automatic mouse traps such as the Ketch-All® and Victor Tin Cat®, which are available from some hardware and farm supply stores. These traps work on the principle that mice will enter small holes without hesitation. The Ketch-All® even has a wind-up spring that powers a rotating mechanism and when triggered, the mechanism entraps mice in a holding compartment.

The Tin Cat® has one-way doors that once mice enter they cannot exit. These traps may catch multiple mice in a single setting, but must be checked and emptied periodically so that mice do not die of starvation or exposure in the traps.

SIGNS OF A MOUSE IN THE HOUSE

The presence of house mice can be determined by a number of signs and usually the droppings are your best clue. Droppings are usually found along runways, in feeding areas and near their shelter. Telling the difference between mouse droppings and those of certain insects are sometimes difficult.

Mouse droppings are about ¼ inch long while those of cockroaches are usually somewhat smaller and under a magnifying glass show distinct longitudinal ridges and squared-off ends. Bat droppings contain insect fragments and are more easily crushed between the fingers.

Gnawing is sometimes visible on doors, ledges, in corners, on wallpaper, on stored materials or on other surfaces. If you spot fresh accumulations of wood shavings, insulation and other gnawed material, this will indicate active infestations.

Nests frequently are found when cleaning garages, closets, attics, basements, and outbuildings where mice are present. They consist of fine, shredded fibrous materials also odors may indicate the presence of house mice. They have a characteristic musky odor, which is a positive indication that house mice are present, and this odor can be used to differentiate their presence from that of rats.

One excellent method to detect the presence of mice is to make nontoxic tracking-dust patches of flour or baby powder at 20 to 30 foot intervals throughout the house. The number of patches showing tracks after 12-24 hours and the number of tracks in each patch, indicate the size of the population. House mice, unlike rats, never travel too far from their nests or shelter and the percentage of patches showing tracks is a good indicator of the relative size and distribution of the mouse population.

RATS

General Information
A rat can fall 50 feet and land on its feet with no injury and squeeze through a hole that is the size of a quarter. They can also tread water for 3 days without a life vest and survive an atomic blast if they are not at ground zero.

RAT FACTS
➢ Rats have very poor vision and to compensate for this, a red or pink eyed rat often weaves its head side to side adding "motion" to see better. They also don't see in color.
➢ Rats prefer to have cage mates and it is possible to have a number of female or male rats together, however, be very careful when introducing a new rat.
➢ While it's nice to have both female and male rats, be wary of letting them play together since rats can complete the entire courting ritual and the whole romantic relationship in about two seconds.
➢ Male rats make better "lap" pets and prefer to sit and have their ears scratched by a human friend. Female rats are very curious and love to explore and play games. Both male and female make great companion pets.
➢ Rats can eat chocolate unlike dogs, which get sick.
➢ Rats can also eat smaller pets, even a small mouse. Rats are omnivores, and have enough predatory instinct left in them to consider birds, fish and even some smaller rodents as snack food.
➢ The oils in cedar and pine are toxic to rats and should not be used in their bedding materials.
➢ A rat's temperature is regulated though its tail. A really hot rat will lie on its back and "sweat" through the soles of its feet.
➢ A group of rats is called a mischief.

- Red discharge from a rat's nose or eyes is usually porphyrin, not blood. Unlike blood, porphyrin is flourescent under UV light and is produced in glands behind the rat's eyes. Overproduction of this discharge can be caused by stress or illness.
- A happy rat will produce chatter or grind its teeth. The chattering teeth usually results in "vibrating" eyes, caused by the lower jawbone pressing the backs of the eyes. This is a good sign, regardless of how it looks.
- It is unlikely you will ever catch rabies from a rat.
- Rats will bathe themselves, usually about six times a day or more. A rat's saliva has some pink pigmentation, which can cause a light-colored rat to look discolored.
- Rats have bellybuttons.
- A rat's fur smells like grape soda.
- Rats can be trained to do simple tricks.
- Rats can train humans to do simple tricks.

RODENT POISON THAT IS HARMLESS TO HUMANS
The following ingredients will be needed:

2	**Ounces of barium carbonate**
½	**Ounce of granulated sugar**
½	**Pound of bread crumbs**

Place All the ingredients into a bowl and mix well then add a small amount of water to dampen and allow the mixture to be made into small balls that can be placed out for the rodents.

DON'T BE A MISER WITH THE TRAPS
Trapping is the best method of getting rid of mice and rats. If you have decided to trap the mice, use plenty of traps*: just keep them away from pets and children.* You can bait the traps with cotton balls, which attract the females who are nest building or peanut butter, which they really like. If you want to give them a real treat mix the peanut butter with rolled oats and add a raisin. Remember, mice travel along the edges of the wall.

Don't set the traps for a day or two, just set them out, this really fakes them out and you will get instant results when you do set them with bait.

Other foods that work well in traps are gumdrops and dried fruit. If you are bothered by Norway rats just feed them hot dogs in the trap.

BORDERING ON THE INSANE
In Cleveland, Ohio there is still an old law on the books that prohibits catching mice without a license.

THE MOUSE ALLERGY
Rodents and especially mice are allergic to oil of peppermint and will not frequent a property where they can smell it. If you place a few drops of oil of peppermint on a piece of cotton and place it anywhere you feel that there is a mouse problem you will never see them again. Use only the "real" oil of peppermint not peppermint extract for the best results. You can also plant peppermint in your garden to keep all types of rodents away from the plants. They are also repelled by camphor and pine tar.

SOUND OFF
Devices that emit ultrasonic sound waves have not been found to work very efficiently on rodents.

THE CAT'S MEOW
A sure fire method of getting rid of rodents is to place a few drops of "Nepeta" or catnip oil on a cotton ball and place it anywhere you have a problem.

CATCHING THE FAMILY PET MOUSE OR HAMSTER
Take a large bowl and butter the inside to make it real slippery. Place a piece of cheese in the bottom and set up a ramp with a piece of wood, tongue depressor or ? The mouse will go for the bait and will not be able to get out.

HIRE A RAT TO CHASE MICE
Rats hate mice and given the chance will run them down and kill them for you. If you don't mind a few rats around you will not have any mice. This is not a great way to get rid of mice.

KILLER MASHED POTATOES
If you leave a bowl of potato flakes and a small bowl of water where the mice can get to them, they will eat the flakes and drink the water.

The flakes will expand in their stomachs and their stomach will burst killing them.

CEMENT THEM IN
A non-toxic poison for rats and mice is to place a dish containing cornmeal and dry cement mixed together in an easy location for them to find. If you place a bowl of water near the dish it will make the rodents stomachs set up faster and turn to solid cement.

WILL NOT WORK ON MEXICAN MICE
Mice tend to damage plant bulbs, especially in the spring. To reduce the amount of damage mix together ½ ounce of Tabasco Sauce™ or other hot sauce in 1 pint of water, add ½ teaspoon of Ivory Liquid Soap™ and 1 teaspoon of cayenne pepper. Place the mixture into a spray bottle and spray around the base of the plants.

IT'S BARBECUE TIME
If you are lucky enough to locate an active rodent burrow, drop some lighted barbecue charcoal briquettes down the burrow. The carbon monoxide should kill the rodents. You can also drop a few pieces of dry ice in the burrow and the carbon dioxide given off will kill the rodents.

REPEL WITH GROUND COVERS
There are a few ground covers that rodents do not like to live in or be around. These include adjuga, carpet bugle, cape weed, chamomile, Indian rock strawberry and creeping speedwell.

DOGS ARE GREAT RATTERS
Dogs are better at catching rats than most cats. In fact, the rat terrier was named for the fact that it was a great rat catcher.

HIRE SOME BARN OWLS
New York City had such a rat problem that they actually built special nesting boxes for barn owls to attract them. A family of 6 barn owls can consume as many as 16 or more rats in one night. This didn't work too well because the nesting boxes were stolen.

PLANTS TO THE RESCUE

Rodents will avoid certain plants that give off repulsive scents. These include daffodils, hyancinths and scillia.

GOPHERS

GOPHER FACTS

The biggest pest gopher is the pocket gopher; which has fur-lined pockets in their cheeks, which they utilize to carry food back to their nest for storage. Their favorite food is alfalfa.

The gopher is often confused with the mole and vole since its habitat overlaps and they have similar eating habits. The control methods are different for these three species causing many people to misidentify their pest and use improper techniques in their effort to get rid of them.

Gophers push out the soil they excavate from the burrow they are building in a fan shape radiating away from their burrow opening. They use both their claws and teeth to dig, pushing the soil behind them with their hind claws then they flip over in a somersault motion and push the soil out of the burrow with their forefeet and chest. One gopher can dig a burrow system that consists of up to 200 yards of tunnel a year moving as much as two tons of soil.

Moles build a volcano-shaped with their entrance in the center. The moles entrance is usually plugged up.

> Pocket gophers never hibernate and are active all year.
> They are most active in their burrow building during the spring through fall, while some species will be less productive during the summer months.
> Their teeth can grow up to 14 inches per year.
> Studies have shown that gophers are active all day long
> The pocket gopher's burrow system will usually consist of a main burrow with a number of branches. Systems found to be linear rather than branched are believed to belong to male gophers searching for a mate.

- Burrow diameters tend to be around 3-4 inches; areas larger than 4 inches are believed to be resting or feeding areas.
- The nesting area of the pocket gopher will be lined with grass and usually some other plant debris that the gopher has found and formed into a ball.
- Some burrows can be as deep as 5-6 feet underground.
- Pocket gophers usually live alone. The exception to this rule occurs during mating season and when the female is raising her young.
- Gophers that live in the more northern locations generally have 1 litter per year. Pocket gophers that live in southern areas usually have 2 litters per year.
- California gophers may breed year-round.
- Litter sizes can vary from 1 to 10 but the average is 3 or 4 young per litter.
- The teeth of the pocket gopher, is continually growing to accommodate the constant wear and tear upon them.
- Gophers can exert a force of up to 18,000 pounds per square inch with their bite.
- Gophers enjoy feasting on your plants, vegetables, tree roots and anything else they can get their teeth into that grows with roots.

FEED THEM, FEED THEM

If you provide them with enough food such as planting annual grains as a buffer strip to protect your crops they may not feed on your crop. If you do not want to plant grains, try a buffer area of bare ground or a barrier of six inches of very coarse gravel.

SMELLY SOLUTION

The following ingredients will be need:

1	Teaspoon of oil of peppermint
1	Teaspoon of chili powder
½	Ounce of Tabasco Sauce™
1	Pint of cold tap water
	Cotton balls

Place all the ingredients into a medium bowl and mix well. Place about 10 drops of the solution on a cotton ball and place the cotton ball anywhere a rodent problem exists or drop the cotton ball down a gopher or mole hole.

DOWN SOUTH REMEDY
Gophers and moles do not like hominy grits. Place the grits down the hole and it will act as a stomach irritant. Any instant grain will also make them very ill and wanting to leave your property and head for the nearest rodent emergency room.

HAIR-RAISING
If you want to get rid of gophers without killing them, just drop human hair down their tunnels. Keep placing the hair in all their new tunnels until they get tired of digging tunnels in your yard and move to your neighbor's yard.

THE OLD SMELLY HERB TRICK
Place 3-4 drops of oil of peppermint (not the extract) on cotton balls and drop the cotton ball down all the entrances to the gopher or mole holes. They are allergic to peppermint and will leave your property or sneeze themselves to death. Citronella works well too if you can't find oil of peppermint. You can also place the product "Deer Off™" on the cotton balls to irritate them. Other oils work well too, such as pennyroyal, citronella and lavender.

GERMAN GOPHER ROCKS
These are lava rocks that have been soaked in a garlic and onion solution that will smell up tunnels to such a degree that the gophers and moles pack their bags and head for the neighbor's yard. The rocks are buried about 6-inches deep in areas where you have plants that they are feeding on. Depending on the amount of rain or watering in the area the rocks will remain effective for 4-12 months. They are sold as "Rodent Rocks™."

MARK THEIR TERRITORY
When you find gopher or mole holes the first step is to place a small flag at every entrance. Purchase an injector tool from your garden supply house to be used with a mixture that will be sprayed into their holes. Hopefully you have found all the holes. The mixture is as follows:

1	**Pound of cayenne pepper or ground very hot chilies**
¼	**Pound of garlic powder**

Place the mixture into the injector and spray into every tunnel and cover with a rock or brick. Best to cover all holes before you start spraying, then open them up one at a time and spray them then replace the cover. Try not to water the area for 24 hours after the treatment.

SMELLY CACKLEBERRIES
If you leave some eggs out of the refrigerator for about 2-3 weeks, they will have high hydrogen sulfide content from the chemicals that break down. The smell of rotten eggs is very offensive to gophers and moles and they will not appreciate your dropping these eggs into their living quarters or tunnels.

PLANT WIRE IN YOUR GARDEN
If you have a problem with gophers every season, it may be best to lay a layer of aviary wire (about ¼ inch mesh) about 6-inches underground. You can also bury ½ inch galvanized wire fencing mesh about 2 feet underground as a barrier. The wire must come all the way to the surface to be effective.

A SCARY SIGHT
Colored wine bottles have been used very effectively when placed underground around the garden. The gophers and moles see their reflection and get scared and run away.

NATURAL PLANT BARRIERS
If you plant a number of garlic and onion plants around the garden it will repel the gophers and moles. They prefer areas that do not contain plants that are offensive to them.

RENT-A-SNAKE

 Gopher snakes love to chase and eat gophers and moles. They are not poisonous and many people keep them as pets. Your local pet store should have a gopher snake that you can just drop down the gopher or mole hole. You will probably not have another problem for a long time.

GOPHER-PROOF HEDGE

Gopher purge (Uphorbia lathyrus) is a plant that contains pods each containing three seeds. The plant is a natural repellant to gophers and moles and all other burrowing animals. The roots are so poisonous to them as well as humans that it will eliminate the problem in short order. Do not get the white milky substance on your hands or face: if you do best to wash it off immediately. It is usually planted as a hedge around gardens and used mainly on the east coast of the United States.

BUY A BLACK HOLE

A Black Hole™ is a circular trap with a hole in the end. An apple attached to a piece of string is used and is very effective for catching gophers. There are a number of traps made to trap gophers and moles but the Black Hole™ seems to be the best.

POWERFUL NATURAL SUPPLEMENT

One of the most effective gopher and mole killers is vitamin D or actually D_3. D_3 is a form of vitamin D that's upsets calcium metabolism in burrowing animals and eventually kills them. D_3 is safe for humans and animals making it an excellent gopher and mole killer.

WATCH 'EM RUN

The following ingredients will be needed:

1	**Ounce of peppermint oil**
¼	**Ounce of cayenne pepper**

Place the ingredients in a small bowl and mix. Dip a cotton ball in the mixture and drop the cotton ball down the gopher or mole hole. You will never see those critters again.

THIS WILL GIVE THEM THE RUNS
Mix one cup of castor oil and 3 tablespoons of ivory liquid soap in 1 gallon of water and pour some down every hole and around their areas. You can use a sprayer if you wish. Apply this mixture early in the morning of a real hot day for the best results.

AYE CHIHUAHUA
Drop a habanero or Serrano chili down the gopher of mole hole and you will never see them again. They will dig to China to get away from it.

BOMBS AWAY
There are few commercial products that can be used if all else fails. Commercial mole smoke bombs are available through garden supply houses. The mole, however, if it gets away will return since the tunnels have not been destroyed and take up housekeeping again.

THEY WON'T HAVE ANY MOTHS IN THEIR HOME
Dropping mothballs works great; they hate the smell and immediately leave their happy home. *Mothballs are also very poisonous to humans as well as all animals.* This would be a very last resort.

CHASE THEM AWAY WITH STATIC
Purchase a small, cheap portable radio and put a long-life battery in it. Wrap the radio in plastic and put on static, then drop it down the gopher hole. If he doesn't change the station you will never see him again.

POISONOUS PLANT

If you plant a few castor bean plants *Euphobia lathyris* around your garden it will either kill the gopher or mole or for them to move to another location. The leaves and stems are poisonous and you need to keep pets and children away from these plants.

There are oils that will eliminate all rodents. Just add 1 cup of castor oil, tea tree oil, cinnamon oil, garlic oil or mineral oil to 1 gallon of warm water. Place a small amount of a natural liquid soap to the mixture and spray the area where they frequent. This is a pretty potent spray. If you want to just scare them away use only 4 drops of the oils in the gallon of water and don't spray directly on them.

GOPHER & MOLE KILLER

The following ingredients will be needed:

4	Ounce of powdered seaweed
2	Ounces of powdered vitamin D_3
2	Ounces of any vegetable powder

 Place all the ingredients in a small plastic container and mix well. Rodents have difficulty regulating their calcium absorption and the vitamin will eventually kill them off. Just place a small amount of the mixture inside a small piece of any vegetable (potato,etc.) by

THIS WILL NOT DOUBLE THEIR PLEASURE

Gophers love Juicy Fruit gum. Just drop a stick or two down the gopher hole and they will eat it and plug up their intestinal tract. It is best to use gloves when unwrapping and handling the gum to avoid the smell of humans.

SOUNDS FISHY

This will drive out moles and gophers immediately. They can't stand the smell of fish and especially rotting fish. Grandpa had an old trick that worked every time he saw a gopher or mole hole. He would drop a fish head down the hole and never saw the gopher again. This irritates them into an instant move on to less odoriferous areas.

SKIP THE FLOODING

I remember cartoons where the gopher was flooded out with a hose poked into his tunnel. While this may work it may also collapse the tunnels in your yard and make a big mess to re-do the yard.

LIGHT 'EM UP

This one really makes them mad. Close off all their tunnel openings and just leave one open for a few minutes. Drop a lighted highway flare down the tunnel and no more gophers or moles.

RATTLE THEM

Place a stick into the ground near one of their tunnels and attach a rattling pinwheel to the stick. The vibrations from the pinwheel will drive them batty. Gophers are extremely sensitive to ground vibrations.

BUY A GO'PHER™

The Go'pher™ is sold in garden shops and emits an ultrasonic noise. It is a battery, operated unit and the sound: cannot be heard by humans and most animals. It will also keep moles and voles away. The device is advertised to keep areas up to 1000 square feet clear of these varmints.

SQUILLS TO THE RESCUE

Gophers hate areas where there are scilla bulbs (squills) planted. These flowering bulb-type ornamentals have grassy leaves and clusters of flowers on the top of long stems. They are easy to grow and if you border you garden it will keep all gophers away.

MOLES/VOLES

A TUNNELING NUISANCE

Moles are great at tunneling with their powerful claws on their front feet. Moles are not a member of the rodent family; however, they are included in this chapter since all the deterrents used for gophers apply to them as well. They normally prefer to live on insects, but when the insects are intermingled with the root system of a plant, they will eat both the insect and the plant's roots.

Their favorite bug is the grub and if you can control the grub population you will probably be able to control the mole population in your yard.

Spraying your yard in early spring for fleas will eliminate the majority of the grub population and reduce the overall number of insects for moles to feed on. Many different types of methods have been tried to remove moles including; smoke bombs, high-pressure water, poisons, rat bait, hand grenades and dynamite.

Because moles expend a high degree of energy they cannot survive more than a few hours without food.

MOLE FACTS

- ➤ Moles are active by day and by night, almost continuously digging their tunnels, making their bests and looking for food. They are active for about 4 hours at a time then rest for 4 hours.
- ➤ A mole will die of starvation if it does not eat every few hours.
- ➤ It finds food by running along its tunnels and consuming any earthworms, beetle larvae, slugs, etc., which have fallen from the walls.
- ➤ A mole eats about least half its own body weight a day.
- ➤ When earthworms are very plentiful, during autumn and winter, the mole stores them by biting off their heads and pushing them into the ground saving them for eating later.
- ➤ When tunneling, a mole will use one front foot to push the soil upwards forming a molehill while it braces the other, and the hind feet, firmly against the tunnel walls. The long claws on the front feet help it to dig.
- ➤ A mole can run backwards through tunnels and turn around by doing a somersault. Its fur lies backwards or forwards so that it does not become stuck against the tunnel walls when they squeeze through them.
- ➤ The eyes of the mole are very tiny and they do not see very well, but sight is not important to a mole living in darkness for most of the time.
- ➤ Moles do not have a good sense of smell or hearing, however, it is extremely sensitive to touch and can sense vibrations in the soil around it.

- The mole has sensitive whiskers help it to find its way about and detect food and water; it is also assisted by thousands of very sensitive, tiny hairs which cover its long nose.
- Moles are sometimes seen above ground but usually only come to the surface to collect nesting material and to look for food when the soil is dry.
- Moles emerge mainly at night but they are still vulnerable to predators; some mammals find them distasteful but many are eaten by barn owls.
- The mole is very often confused with gophers and voles due to habitat overlap and similar eating habits.
- Control methods differ for these three species; many people misidentify their target and often use improper techniques in their abatement efforts.
- Moles are not rodents, they are insectivores, and related to shrews and bats.
- Moles never hibernate.
- Mole mounds are shaped like a volcano and can reach heights of up to two feet tall.
- Moles can dig up to 18 feet of surface tunnels per hour.
- The "tentacles" on the nose of the star-nosed mole is probably the most sensitive sensory organ of any mammal. The star-nosed mole utilizes these "tentacles" to continually monitor its surroundings.
- The star-nosed mole is extremely active throughout the winter. It has been known to form tunnels through snow and even swim under the ice of frozen ponds.

VOLES

General Information

There are 70 species of voles, which vary in size 3½ to 7 inches long. They have rounded bodies with gray or brown coats, blunt muzzles, small ears, and short tails. Most of the species are considered pests. Several species live in artic habitats and are referred to as artic voles. Voles normally produce 3 to 6 vole litters per year averaging 3 to 6 babies per litter. Voles live in small colonies of a few to 300 individuals.

Some voles are strictly herbivores while others are omnivores and will eat grasses, bark, leaves, seeds, nuts, berries, fungi, roots, bulbs, tubers, snails and insects. They create runways in grasses and vegetation on the surface of the ground and are able to dig underground burrows. The tunnels provide them with protection from predators and from the weather.

The meadow vole is one of the most common while the salt marsh vole is bigger than the meadow vole. Red-backed voles spend much of their time in shrubs and bushes. The water vole lives in Europe and Western Asia and is a large, semi-aquatic vole that looks like a small muskrat. The bank vole is the smallest vole species in the UK and has short hamster-like noses.

Predators that like to feast on voles include hawks, eagles, owls, weasels, cats, foxes, coyotes, badgers, skunks, bobcats, and snakes.

VOLE FACTS

➤ In North America voles may be known as field mice or meadow mice.
➤ Voles can have large population fluctuations, anywhere from 16 to 400 voles per acre.
➤ The red-backed vole has a reddish stripe from its forehead to rump.
➤ Voles are mostly nocturnal; however, some are out more in the daytime in the winter looking for food.
➤ Prairie voles are monogamous and mate for life.
➤ The vole is often confused with the mole or gopher due to habitat overlap and similar eating habits, however, control methods differ for these three species; many people misidentify their target and often use improper techniques in their abatement efforts.
➤ Some species of vole can be found at elevations of up to 12,000 ft.
➤ Voles are not very sanitary animals and piles of feces will usually be found throughout their burrow.
➤ Most voles rarely live more than 1-2 years.
➤ Meadow voles are very aggressive and will attack and bite if cornered or captured.

Use the same methods for voles as mentioned for gophers and moles.

MUSIC TO GOPHER BY

Gophers and moles do not like loud sounds. If you place a cheap transistor radio playing hard rock into their domain you will never see them again. They are very sensitive to sound waves.

GRUB CONTROL

If you control the grubs on your property, chances are that you will never have a mole around.

WHERE'S THE CAT

Used kitty litter placed into the mole's tunnel will cause them to move on to your neighbors' property very quickly.

YUK.........................

Place an ear of fresh corn painted with roofing tar in their tunnel. They hate the odor of tar and will look for a new home in your neighbor's yard.

GET 'EM ON THE RUN

Drop a few Ex-Lax™ squares down their hole. You will never see them again! Works with a hot pepper as well!

PORCUPINE

General Information:

The porcupine is also known as the **"quill pig"** and is a member of the rodent family. It has about 30,000 spiny quills, which are barbed at the head. The quills cover the entire body with the exception of the underneath side and the head. They like thin tree bark, leaves and buds but have a sweet tooth and will eat corn, melon and berries if they can get them. They have been known to ruin berry bushes by stripping the bark off the stems and trunks. If your dog has a run in with a porcupine it would be best to get the dog to the vet as soon as possible. If shocking doesn't work you will have to trap them.

SHOCK THEM

Porcupines are good climbers and you will need a chicken wire fence about 2 feet high with an electric wire on top just a few inches above it. Angle the fence at a 65^0 angle away from the garden for the best results.

PORCUPINE FACTS

> Porcupines possess a special ability to retain nitrogen from their food and not allow it to pass through. This is what will allow them to survive the winter on a steady diet of bark.
> They have even been compared to deer and other ruminant animals because of this trait.
> Porcupines will constantly lose weight in the winter and it is estimated that they lose nearly 30% of the body weight during the cold winter months.
> Porcupines that live in the Rockies carry with them over 40 wood ticks that can carry the Colorado Tick Virus. They hardly ever spread the virus since only adult ticks live on the porcupine and adults do not carry the virus.
> Porcupines have been seen falling out of trees fairly often and have occasionally been impaled by their own quills.

> Newborn porcupines are heavier than grizzly bear cubs at birth.
> Porcupines mate in the fall then give birth in the spring. They have the longest gestation period of any rodent.
> A baby porcupine is called a porcupette.
> Porcupines waddle around, however, may actually erupt into a gallop when frightened.
> Porcupines are not listed endangered but have been eradicated from certain areas of the United States.

Quill Facts:

> A porcupine's quills are inter-dispersed with its normal hair.
> They have a light, spongy center.
> Porcupine quills do not contain poison.
> The Porcupine quills are really a third type of hair found on the animal. They also have very course guard hairs and dense, bristly undercoats.

- American Indians used the quills of the porcupine for hair brushes and decorations
- The quills have an oily coating on them, which allows for easier penetration into an attacker. The quill's coating is much slicker during the summer when their diet is more nutrient rich.
- The quills also have an antibiotic property in case the porcupine accidently gets stuck.
- Porcupine quills can be up to 5 inches long.
- The quills are lightly-colored in contrast to the animal's otherwise black fur in order to appear striking and serve as a visual warning to potential predators.
- Quills from a porcupine can vary in length. The shorter quills are usually found near its head, while the longer quills can be found at the rear of the animal.
- Muscles attached to the quill follicles allow the porcupine to raise and lower them. When threatened, they raise their quills, making themselves appear larger while also "arming" the quills in case of attack.
- Baby porcupines are born with soft spines, which will actually harden within an hour.
- Porcupines are timid and they primarily use their spines for defense.
- When threatened and they are unable to escape, the porcupine flips so its rear (and longer spines) face the attacker.
- Porcupines may also jump towards an aggressor.
- Porcupines never shoot their quills. They do not have this capability.
- Quills are easily detached from the porcupine when they impale an object or animal.
- Lost quills will grow back within a few months.
- A patch of quills on the lower back grows atop a scent gland and when threatened, the porcupine can release a pungent odor, while not as bad as a skunk, it will force you move away very fast.
- Porcupines can accidentally stick themselves. This usually happens if they fall out of a tree.
- The best way to remove a porcupine quill is to simply pull it out, but be sure not break the quill.

TRAPPING THE QUILL PIG

The best method of removing a porcupine is to trap the animal. Trapping a porcupine is best done by a professional with the proper traps, tools, and experience.

Most large exterminator companies should be able to help or contact the local humane society. You need to protect yourself and your property. Once the animal is caught it can be released a distance from your property.

SHREWS

SHREWS ARE SHREWD
You have to be crafty to catch a shrew, but the best method is a mousetrap. The bait needs to be  peanut butter and rolled oats and if you add just a hint of bacon grease or hamburger it will increase the effectiveness.

SHREW FACTS
- Ancient Egyptians believed that the shrew contained the spirit of darkness.
- Shrews have also been thought of as the beast god that would protect stored grains from rats and mice.
- Shrew is derived from the Middle English word "shrewe," which translates to mean an evil person.
- There are over 300 difference species of shrews worldwide.
- Short-tailed shrews are so close in physical appearance the only way to tell them apart is from their range and by chromosome count.
- North America's pygmy shrew is the second smallest mammal in the world.
- Shrews live on every continent except Australia and Antarctica.
- There are some species of shrew that live in water habitats.
- There are some mammals with "shrew" in their name that are not actually shrews, which include Elephant shrews and porcupine shrews.
- Shrews have extremely fast heart beat that averages 700 beats per minute. With a heart beating that fast the animals are easily startled and can have heart failure. Shrews have even been known to drop dead of fright after a loud burst of thunder.
- The Short-tailed Shrews have a poisonous bite! They have glands in their teeth that secrete a poison that is toxic to smaller mammals such as mice and other shrews, which paralyses them rendering them helpless. This then allows shrews to prey on mammals larger than themselves.

> Shrews excrete a musky smell from scent glands located on the belly and sides. The smell is so foul that while shrews are often killed, they are rarely eaten.

TRAP THE LITLE CRITTERS

The best option would be to use mouse snap traps with an expandable peddle. The traps can be baited with small bits of meat, peanut butter or tuna fish and placed where shrew activity has been noticed. Rat-sized glue boards can be used in places where snap traps are prohibited. Caution should be used when dealing with shrews. Shrews have been known to attack family pets and will bite humans if handled.

SAFE SHREW REMOVAL

There is a safe and easy method to remove shrews that won't harm them. Just sprinkle granules of Shake-Away™ on the ground where they frequent and they will never come back. The product is all-natural and effective without using poisons. It is 100% organic and safe for the family, pets and plants.

ELIMINATION BY THE NUMBERS

Step 1
You will first need to locate the area that the shrews use as a run by looking for fecal matter. Shrews tend to use a few locations as a toilet. Look in and around the garden, near trees and by the sides of the house.

Step 2
You will need a gallon jar. Dig a hole for your gallon jar. The hole should be deep enough so that the lip of the jar is at the surface of the hole. Place a small amount of grass over the pit trap to hide its location.

Step 3
Check the pit trap in the morning before the temperature gets too hot. Check the trap four times within a 24 hour period for the shrew.

Step 4
Take the jar out of the ground once a shrew is caught, being very careful not to get your hand too close to the animal. Some varieties of shrews are venomous. Release the shrew at least 200 yards from the capture lo

SQUIRRELS/CHIPMUNKS

General Squirrel Information

Squirrels belong to the order "Rodentia," which has 1650 species and is the largest group of mammals. This group also comprises 40% of all present day mammal species. There are over 365 species of squirrels in seven families, which include the common tree squirrel, ground squirrel and flying squirrel. Plus there are many squirrel-like mammals such as gophers, groundhogs and prairie dogs.

Squirrels are by far the most active in the late winter when their mating season begins. The males will be out chasing females as well as chasing off other rivals for the female's attention. This ritual of chasing occurs in the tree tops at a very fast speed and while they perform some of the most courageous acrobatics imaginable.

The pregnancy period varies from 33 days in the small species of squirrels to up to 60 days for the larger species such as the gray and fox squirrels. Squirrels are usually born early in the spring with the average litter consisting of 3-4. A female squirrel always chooses the strongest male during mating season; however, they rarely breed with that male again.

Baby squirrels; weigh about one ounce at birth and is about one inch long. They have no hair or teeth and are blind for the first 6-8 weeks. Gray squirrels can be seen in many colors; however, shades of gray are the most common followed by shades of tan and brown. It is not that unusual to see a pure white and pure black squirrel with both being related to the gray squirrel.

In summer squirrels are usually most active two to three hours after sunrise then they will relax the rest of the afternoon and become active again about two hours before sunset. Squirrels will begin nesting well before dark and will rarely leave the nest during dark hours. During the winter, squirrels will complete their activities between dawn and mid-day then remain in or around the nest until the next day.

SQUIRREL FACTS

- ➤ During winter storms or very cold weather squirrels may not leave their nest for days.
- ➤ The tree squirrel does not hibernate!
- ➤ The gray squirrels diet consists of nuts, seeds and occasionally fruit.
- ➤ Squirrels will also eat bird eggs, bugs and even a road kill if there is no other food source available.
- ➤ Gray squirrels require some salt in its diet and usually find salt in the soil along roads where snow and ice were melted with salt.
- ➤ The adult squirrel normally lives alone; however, they are smart enough in cold weather to share their nest with other squirrels to conserve body heat. As the temperature becomes warmer, the guests will be on their way.
- ➤ Squirrels eyes are located high and on each side of their head allowing them a wide field of vision, without turning their head.
- ➤ Squirrels will chew on tree branches to sharpen and clean their teeth. This is why you may see small tree branches on the ground around large trees. However, they will also chew on power lines for the same reason, which has caused many power outages and a number of crispy critters.
- ➤ A squirrel's brain is about the size of a black walnut.
- ➤ The average adult squirrel consumes about a pound of food a week to maintain their active lifestyle.
- ➤ Squirrels can communicate with each other with a series of chirps. The frequency and duration of the sounds can communicate everything from laughter to alarm.
- ➤ The sounds when used in conjunction with tail gestures form the basis for squirrel communication.
- ➤ If a squirrel is living in your attic, the only practical way to remove them is by trapping.
- ➤ Squirrels break the shell of a nut with its teeth then clean the nut by licking it or rubbing the nut on its face before it is buried. By doing this, they apply a scent to the nut, which helps the squirrel find it later, even under a foot of snow.
- ➤ The sweat glands of a gray squirrel are found on their feet between the foot pads and on their paws between the toes. When excited a squirrel will leave wet sweat tracks on a dry surface. The track will contain a scent and is used to mark the trees in their territory.

- When a squirrel senses danger, its first instinct is to stand totally still. If they are on the ground they will race to the closest tree or other climbable object and escape. If it is in a tree, it will circle the trunk with its body pressed tightly to the bark before climbing to gain a good foothold.
- The male tree squirrel takes twice as long as the female, to groom itself and are the cleanest animal in the rodent family.
- Squirrels teeth grow continuously with their incisor's growing about six inches per year; however, they remain short due to the constant wear they receive.
- The most common type of squirrel bite is usually a result of feeding a squirrel by hand. You should never hold the food between your fingers or chances are very good you will be bitten. Since a squirrel's eyes are always looking for predators, they rarely focus on what they are eating.

General Chipmunk information

There are chipmunk facts, which apply to all chipmunks, such as striped faces, cheek pouches, and vertical tail posturing; however, there are a number of different species, each species having its own unique facts. For instance, in North America, there are 22 species of chipmunk. Most of which are native to California, with a few species found in neighboring states.

The fact is that only 9 of the 22 species are native to regions outside of California. California does have several species, which are found only in small coastal or high in the Sierra Mountains. The Alpine chipmunk is only found in the Sierras at altitudes between 7,500 and 13,000 feet. The Yellow-cheeked chipmunk is only found in a couple of California counties.

Palmer's chipmunk is found only in the mountains near Las Vegas, Nevada and at the other extreme, the Eastern chipmunk is found in most parts of eastern North America and from Nova Scotia to Louisiana. Hardly any chipmunks are found in the Rocky Mountain Range, the Sierras and from New Mexico into Central Canada.

CHIPMUNK FACTS
- Chipmunks are members of the rodent family and are very closely related to squirrels.

- Chipmunks are generally much smaller than squirrel's, which makes it easy to tell the difference between chipmunks and squirrels and this is possible even in the case of young, small squirrels.
- A significant feature of chipmunks is that all species have stripes on their faces and squirrels do not.
- Chipmunks have pouches in their cheeks for storing food similar to hamsters and can take food to their burrows or to hide in caches.
- Squirrels do not have cheek pouches.
- A sure way to tell a chipmunk from a squirrel is just to chase one, or scare one away. Squirrels run away with its tail in parallel to the ground, chipmunks run with its tail held vertically.

- Most chipmunks burrow in the ground or live in rocky outcroppings, but some species nest in trees and may take over a bird's nests.
- Male chipmunks rarely care for their young; however, the males of several species are quite attentive to their young.
- Chipmunks will usually share their food supply with other chipmunks, but will be extremely territorial when it comes to their immediate surroundings, especially near their nest or burrow.
- The range of a chipmunk averages about 3 acres.
- The reason chipmunk's store so much food is that they don't put on very much weight as winter approaches, so when hibernating, they need to wake up occasionally and have a small meal to keep them going.

STOP TULIP DECAPITATING

If you mix up a batch of squirrel deterrent spray, it will keep the cute little critters away from your budding plants, which they enjoy munching on.

Boil 1 quart of water and remove from the heat as soon as it starts to boil, then add 2 tablespoons of cayenne pepper and ½ teaspoon of Tabasco Sauce.

Allow it to stand for about 2-3 hours making sure it is very cool before placing the mixture into a sprayer and spraying the stems of the plants as soon as the buds appear.

STOP THE FURNITURE CHEWER
Some squirrels like to chew on legs of wooden garden furniture. To stop them, just paint the legs with a watery solution of hot sauce, then wipe clean. This will leave enough hot residue to discourage them.

PROVIDING YOU HAVE A PUTTY TAT
Place a very small amount of used cat litter around the base of the budding plants. This will deter squirrels and chipmunks from digging up bulbs. Also works well on all flowering plants in areas where you have a rodent problem. They think that there is a cat nearby waiting to pounce on them.

WRAP YOUR TRUNKS
Placing a metal band around tree trunks works great as long as there are no other trees for the squirrel to go from one tree to the other. The band should be a smooth metal and at least 2-feet wide and 6-8 feet off the ground.

USE STEEL WOOL
If you have any openings into the attic from the outside it would be best to place steel wool to keep the squirrel and other critters from setting up housekeeping there.

If they are already in the attic then place a heavy piece of rubber to block the opening only allowing them to exit and not enter.

TRAPPING SQUIRRELS
Traps can be purchased in most hardware stores or garden supply centers. The bait needs to be peanut butter, nuts, seeds or their favorite, vanilla extract.

PETER PIPER'S PLATES
When squirrels become a pest and get into your fruit trees, try tying some "real" aluminum pie plates to the tree to scare them off. Place them on the lower limbs of all trees.

WHOOOOPS

If you place a layer of lubricating gel around the trunk of the tree about one-foot wide the squirrels will not be able to climb the tree. The only problem here is if you have another tree that you have not done this too in close proximity to the tree you want to protect. It is best to do this on all trees.

TANGLE THEM UP

If you want to discourage them, just place some Tanglefoot™ around the trunk of the tree. This sticky substance will deter them from climbing the tree.

WEIRD BARRACADE

If you can get a bunch of 1 quart plastic milk bottles, ones with the little handles, just place a string through the handles and hang them around the trunk of the trees you are having a problem with.

If you can't find enough quart ones use the gallon size and just cut off the tops and nail them on with the open side down around the trunk of the tree touching each other.

A BLOODY GOOD IDEA

If you sprinkle blood meal around the borders of your garden where you are having a squirrel problem it will deter them.

HOT PEPPER SPRAY

If you prepare a spray made from pureed hot peppers and dilute it with water, then add a few drops of Ivory liquid soap and spray it on plants that the squirrels are frequenting it will keep them away.

THIS WILL GIVE THEM THE RUNS

If you puree some red hot peppers and add tablespoon of mineral oil to it then apply it to ears of corn that you are having a problem with to deter squirrels. Just apply the solution to the silk end of the corn.

BAFFLE THEM

Baffles can be placed on trees to stop the squirrels from climbing the tree, however, if other trees are not baffled near the tree they will just jump across.

WOODCHUCKS

General Information:

 These rodents are also known as **"groundhogs"** and can really do a lot of damage in a garden or farm. They are usually found in farms near a wooded area and build burrows that can cause damage to farm vehicles. They hibernate in the winter months. Live off their fat layer and their respiration can fall to only one breath every 5 minutes. Woodchucks only live through 4-5 winters. They burrow 2-5 feet deep and are continually improving their den or building a new one. Horses and other farm animals have often been injured stepping in a woodchuck hole.

Be careful around woodchucks since they can carry rabies and you do not want to be bitten by them. If you do get bitten go to the doctor immediately. If you have a big problem with woodchucks, trapping is the only answer.

In areas that have large quantities of alfalfa or other food crops, woodchucks can grow up to 30 lbs. Woodchucks are excellent diggers with their curved thick claws. They have short tails compared to most other ground dwelling squirrels.

Woodchucks are vegetarians and their diet consists of grasses, clover, garden vegetables, leaves, apples, berries and an occasional dandelion. They are not really omnivorous, but will sometimes eat small animals such as insects and snails if they can't find another food source.

Woodchucks can become almost motionless when alerted to danger and will whistle when alarmed to warn other woodchucks. They are excellent burrowers and use the burrows for sleeping, bringing up their young and hibernating.

Woodchuck burrows usually have between two and five entrances, providing groundhogs their primary means of escape from predators. Burrows are very large and can have as much as 45 feet of tunnels buried up to 5 feet underground, which can pose a serious threat to agricultural and residential development by injuring animals, damaging farm machinery and even undermining building foundations.

Woodchucks run to their burrows when danger is spotted. If the burrow is invaded, the woodchuck is a formidable foe and will tenaciously defend itself with its two large incisors and sharp front claws. Common predators for woodchucks include wolves, coyotes, eagles, large hawks and owls. Young groundhogs are often eaten by snakes but the threat is quickly reduced as they grow larger and become to large for the snakes to eat.

 Woodchucks breed in their second year; however, a small percentage may breed as yearlings. Their breeding season goes from early March to middle or late April. A mated pair will always remain in the same den through the 28-32 day gestation period. However, as birth of the young gets closer in April or May, the male will usually leave the den.

WOODCHUCK FACTS
- ➢ Woodchucks secrete its territorial marking scent through three nipple like anal glands.
- ➢ Female woodchucks have one litter of usually three to five young per year.
- ➢ Woodchucks live for about 6 to 10 years.
- ➢ Woodchucks will climb trees in search of food.
- ➢ Woodchucks have been observed swimming.
- ➢ The woodchuck has earned its nickname "whistle-pig" since it has a tendency to produce a high-pitched whistle when frightened, which it may mix with both barking and chattering noises.
- ➢ Woodchucks hibernate through the winter
- ➢ Woodchucks are rodents, belonging to a species of large ground squirrels known as marmots.
- ➢ Most marmots, such as yellow-bellied and hoary marmots, live in rocky and mountainous areas; however, woodchucks are lowland creatures.
- ➢ They are widely distributed throughout North America and more common in the eastern and central United States. In the west they are only found in Alaska, Alberta, British Columbia and northern Washington.
- ➢ Woodchucks will travel a great distance to a food source.
- ➢ The woodchuck does not "chuck wood."
- ➢ One of the woodchuck's best defense mechanisms is the spraying of a musky odor from its anal glands.

- Woodchucks have the ability to manipulate objects with their paws because of they have a fifth "finger" sometimes referred to as a thumb stump.
- Woodchucks have been found that have all black or all white fur in the wild.

THEY DON'T LIKE THE ALLIUM FAMILY
Woodchucks do not like certain plants of the allium family. These include garlic and onions.

PEPPER SPRAY WORKS
Puree a number of very hot peppers, strain the mixture and add water and a few drops of liquid soap then spray the area where you are having a problem with woodchucks. They hate hot peppers and will leave very quickly.

THE OLD WATER IN GLASS JUG TRICK
Farmer's in the mid-west have a solution to woodchuck problems! They place clear glass jugs filled ¾ full with clear water and seal the top.

They leave the jugs around the areas where the woodchucks like to frequent. Woodchucks are scared of their own reflection and will shy away from these areas.

A LITTLE HERE AND THERE
Just sprinkle blood meal or even talcum powder around a burrow to force the woodchuck to find another location to reside in.

FOR A SERIOUS PROBLEM
If you have a serious problem the best way to solve it if the area is not too big is with a fence. The fence needs to be 3-4 feet high and at least 18 inches deep. If you can electrify the top strand it would help as well as angling the fence 65^0 away from your garden so that they can't climb it easily.

BRRRRRRRRRRRRRRR

If you place dry ice in their tunnel it will cause them to move rather quickly. They do not like the increase of carbon dioxide gas that is released.

CHAPTER 4

MISCELLANEOUS ANIMALS

ALLIGATORS

General Information
The average size of an adult female American alligator is 8.2 feet and the average size for a male is 11.2 feet. However, large males can reach a weight of nearly 1,000 pounds. Both the male and female have an "armored" body with a muscular flat tail. The skin on the back is armored with embedded bony plates. They have four short legs and the front legs have five toes while the back legs have four toes.

Alligators have a long snout with upward facing nostrils at the end, which allows them breathe while the rest of the body remains underwater. The young can be distinguished from adults since they have bright yellow stripes on their tail, whereas adults have dark stripes on the tail.

Female alligators usually live in a small fairly confined area. The males, however, occupy areas larger than two square miles. Both males and females have been known to extend their ranges during the courting and breeding season to find acceptable mates. Young alligators remain in the area where they are hatched and where they can be protected by their mother. After two to three years, they will leave the area in search of food, or are driven out by the larger alligators.

Alligators undergo periods of dormancy when the weather is cold and excavate a depression called a "gator hole" along a waterway and use it during dormancy. In areas where the water level fluctuates, alligators will dig themselves into depressions in the mud that fill with water. The depressions look like tunnels and are often as long as 65 feet and provide protection during extreme hot or cold weather.

The American alligator is found from North Carolina to Florida to the Rio Grande in Texas. Alligators are usually always found in freshwater and in slow-moving rivers.

They are also found in swamps, marshes and lakes. They can only tolerate salt water for a brief period because they do not have salt glands. The American alligator is listed as threatened on the U.S. Endangered Species List because it is very similar in appearance to the American crocodile, which is endangered and hunters are likely to confuse the two species.

Since alligators will feed on almost anything, they pose a minor threat to humans. In Florida, where there is a big alligator population, there were still only five deaths attributed to alligator attacks from 1973 to 1990. Dogs and other smaller pets are also sometimes killed. At a zoo, the American alligator is fed rats, chickens and rabbits.

Both males and females reach sexual maturity when they reach about six feet long, which takes them about 10-12 years. They breed during the night in shallow waters. Males will actually roar to attract females and to ward off other males then the male circles the female and mounts. Courtship starts in April, with mating occurring in early May.

 After they mate, the female builds a nest of vegetation. The nest measures seven to ten in diameter and is two to three feet high then, around late June and early July, the female lays 35 to 50 eggs. The eggs are then covered with the vegetation and remain through the 65-day incubation period. The sex of the juveniles is usually determined by the temperature of the nest. If the temperature is above 93°F (33.8°C) they will be all male, below 86°F (30°C) all will be female, and temperatures in between will produce both sexes.

American alligators can live to about age 50 in the wild and after it is four feet long, they are usually safe from predators except humans and occasionally other alligators.

ALLIGATOR FACTS
- Only two countries on earth have alligators: the United States and China.
- The Chinese alligator has become endangered and lives only in the Yangtze River valley.

- Although alligators have heavy bodies and slow metabolism, they are capable of short bursts of speed that can reach around 30 miles per hour.
- Alligators are opportunistic feeders and will eat almost anything they can catch, which may include fish, insects, snails, lizards, your pet cat or dog and crustaceans.
- The bigger they get, they take progressively larger prey including: larger fish such as gar, turtles, various mammals, birds and other reptiles.
- While alligators are often confused with crocodiles, they belong to two quite separate families and are as different from one another as humans are from chimps.
- As for appearance, one generally rule, is that alligators have U-shaped heads, while crocodiles heads are V-shaped.

ALLIGATOR; GET OUT OF MY POND!
Alligators do not like salt water! They will not remain in salty water for any length of time. However, salting the pond water may kill a number of plants, insects and fish. Best to call a professional to remove them!

ARMADILLOS

General Information
Armadillos are very closely related to sloths and anteaters. Their distinctive armor plating is composed of actual bones, which makes the armadillo fairly inflexible. Its outer "armor" is used more as a deterrent to predators, rather than an actual means of defense. Only the 3-Banded Armadillo can actually roll itself into a ball for protection, the other 19 species use their speed and digging abilities to escape predators.

They have stubby, powerful legs and strong claws, which are designed for digging and they do so constantly. They dig numerous burrows and a number of escape holes and can interlink them with an extensive network of tunnels. Armadillos will dig for food and will probe the ground and rotting trees for insects, grubs and other invertebrates including ants.

Armadillos will eat eggs and even baby birds, mice or other small mammals if they can catch them. It really likes to dig, which has caused the armadillo to be considered destructive pest by humans. However, they will consume insects that cause damage to crops and lawns. Humans, cars and pets tend to reduce the population. However, the 9-Banded Armadillo has increased its range from South America to Kansas.

Armadillos prefer habitats with sandy soils, which is easier to dig through and can be found in grasslands, woodlands, wetlands and even areas of thorny scrub. When it comes to reproducing, the 9-Banded Armadillo is rather unique. After they mate in July, the fertilized egg will remain dormant until November, which is called "delayed implantation." Once implanted, the one egg will divides into genetically identical quadruplets, which will be born 4 months later.

ARMADILLO FACTS

➢ The name armadillo is derived from the Spanish, meaning "little armored one."
➢ Armadillos are one of the few animals who can consume fire ants as part of their diet. This ability can make armadillos very beneficial to humans.
➢ They are both excellent diggers and also good swimmers. Armadillos have been known to hold their breath for up to 6 minutes.
➢ Armadillos have very poor eyesight and are easily startled while foraging for food.
➢ If they find that they can't dig under it, armadillos will climb over it and are quite capable of scaling fences and trees.
➢ Armadillo teeth have no enamel and they have very few teeth, just several peg-like molars.
➢ Similar to most insect eating mammals, armadillos have a very long, sticky tongue and use it to slurp up bugs as quickly as possible.
➢ They also are equipped with strong claws and are able to tear open ant nests. Their cousins are the anteaters, which have very similar tongues and claws.

TRAPPING THE CRITTERS

Armadillo traps are available at most farm supply stores or can sent away for. When you finally catch one, you can either release it to a faraway place or give it to your wildlife protection office for assistance.

SHAKE-AWAY TO THE RESCUE

A great natural method of getting rid of armadillos is to use a 100% natural product that is very effective. Just sprinkle the granules on the ground and no more armadillos. It is safe around children and pets and is not poisonous.

COMMERCIAL AMMONIA PRODUCTS

There are a number of companies that sell ammonia and urine products that will repel armadillos and may be found at farmer's supply stores or garden supply stores.

PEPPER THEM

Purchase a can of cayenne pepper and go into your yard and figure out where the armadillos have been digging then sprinkle the pepper around the area and also around your plants.

HOT, HOT, HOT

Use a hot pepper spray concoction to get rid of armadillos. Allow 1 cup of crushed hot chilies soak in a gallon of water for about a week then place the gallon container in an area where the sun will hit it so the chilies can steep. After a week, strain the mixture and put it in a spray bottle and spray plants and areas where the armadillos have dug in your yard.

HAIR, HAIR

Brush your dog or cat and collect its fur to use in your yard. The fur is likely to blow around, so you might have to repeat the process often. The scent from the animal's hair will repel the armadillo since it will smell the predator and be scared off.

LET YOUR PET HELP YOU!

Allow your dog or cat to urinate in your yard. The urine will act in the same manner as the pet's hair. However, it may also kill a few plants and some grass.

HANG 'EM HIGH

Try hanging strong, scented soap bags from low-lying branches. You can also hang bars of soap from the shrubs, as well. Grind the soap and place it in a mesh-type bag and tie it off with twine then knot the twine to form a loop and hang it from the shrubs or branches. The strong fragrance will provide a deterrent for armadillos.

BADGERS

General Information

The preferred diet of the badger consists of earthworms, grubs, frogs, slugs, snails, mice and lizards, but it will also eat your vegetables, especially carrots, potatoes and sweet corn. The good news is that badger problems are usually seasonal. There are eight different badger species, all belonging to the weasel family. Badgers can be found in North America, Great Britain, Ireland, Scandinavia, China, Japan and Indonesia.

Some badgers prefer to live alone while others will join a clan of 2 to 15 other badgers. Badgers are fiercely protective animals when it comes to their young and have been known to fight an animal as large as a bear or a wolf. In most countries, badgers are now protected, making it illegal to injure, kill or take one out of its habitat.

Badgers have a thick, short neck, short legs and short bushy tail. One of the more distinctive badger facts is that they have a white stripe from the top of their head down to their nose. Badgers can primarily be found in open plains and prairies and rarely come in to urban areas. Male badgers are much larger than the females and can weigh 30 pounds or more.

The honey badger is considered the most, fierce hunter in the desert. Badgers live in burrows that they make by digging with all of their feet, not just the front ones like most animals.

One of the more disturbing badger facts is that they are a food source in China and are readily available in market places because they are not protected there.

BADGER FACTS

- ➢ Badgers have a great sense of smell but very poor eyesight.
- ➢ The diet of a badger is almost anything and can consist of insects, earthworms, grubs, reptiles, fish, birds, mice, squirrels, chipmunks, fruit, roots, porcupines, honey and snakes.
- ➢ One of the most fun badger facts is that they appear intoxicated after they eat rotten fruit, which tends to ferment very fast in their digestive tract.
- ➢ Badgers can live to be 14 years old however, only a few make it that long.
- ➢ American badgers are able to remain underground for 70 days, however, they do not hibernate the way that many animals do.
- ➢ A badger can smell 800 times better than humans.
- ➢ The whiskers around the badger's nose and eyes are very sensitive and help them to dig and find food easily.
- ➢ You can tell a badger's age by the condition of its teeth.
- ➢ Badgers are excellent swimmers.
- ➢ Badger's hair has been used for centuries to produce shaving brushes.
- ➢ A badger can get all of the water that it needs by eating worms since they have very high water content.
- ➢ Badgers will often prey on hibernating animals in the winter.
- ➢ The gestation period for badgers is seven to eight weeks and results in anywhere from two to five cubs being born in either March or April.
- ➢ Badgers can eat more than 200 earthworms in one day.
- ➢ Badgers are the fastest digging animals found anywhere in the world and can dig faster than a human with a shovel. If you need a hole dug fast, hire a badger!
- ➢ A badger's residence is referred to as a sett.
- ➢ Some badgers will use their same burrow every year and will evict another animal.

CHAIN LINK

You can put in a permanent chain link fence; however, it needs to be buried 12-20 inches deep for it to be 100% effective. This should also keep other critters from entering your property.

DON'T FENCE ME OUT!

The only realistic way to stop badgers from entering gardens is to use a small electric fence. While this may sound like a major undertaking it is reasonably simple and less expensive than building a more permanent fence. It has the advantage of being removable and is only necessary during certain times of the year when badgers are being particularly troublesome.

An electric fence can be used to prevent badgers entering the whole garden, so you will need a long fence across all possible points of entry.

BEAVERS

General Information

Beavers are dark brown with a tail that resembles a paddle. A typical beaver can weigh 30-60 pounds. The beaver also has huge front teeth.
The beaver's fur is very thick and oily and basically waterproof. When a beaver is under the surface of a pond, it operates a little like a submarine and closes all hatches. It has a transparent third eyelid, which protects the eye, while still allowing the beaver to see. Special valves close its nostrils and ears, while fur-lined lips keep the beaver from swallowing water, while chewing or carrying wood or moving vegetation beneath the surface.

Beavers are, of course, famous for their teeth, tails, and fur and very highly respected as home builders and dam builders. However, beavers are also known as lumberjacks and are able to fell a fairly good-sized tree in a fairly short period of time.

There are three beaver species, the most common is the American beaver, also called the common or true beaver. The other two species are the called the Eurasian beaver and the mountain beaver.

The American beaver is the second largest rodent in the world, a South American rodent that is not related to the beaver family, is the largest. Beaver life is centered about and around water, where the beaver spends most of its time. Even though it is a good fighter, the beaver is very vulnerable on land since it cannot move swiftly and is in danger of being attacked by wolves, badgers, eagles, bears and other predators.

When possible to escape a predator, the beaver will retreat into the water, where it can better hold its own. If a predator is spotted in the vicinity, the beaver slap its tail on the surface of the water making a very loud sound to serve as a warning to other beavers in the area. Beavers are herbivores and are able to digest woody material, such as hardwood tree bark.

Beavers will consume a variety of other vegetation including many different types of water plants and grasses, leaves and tree roots. They will usually store twigs and branches underwater close to their lodges or dens, so they will have an easy source of food if the water freezes over since their entrances are normally underwater.

BEAVER FACTS
- ➤ Beaver's hind feet are webbed and clawed and their front feet are smaller, but not webbed.
- ➤ The beaver's large front teeth or incisors protrude in front of their lips, which helps them cut and chew submerged wood without getting water in their mouths.
- ➤ Their broad tail functions acts as a rudder, helping them to maneuver large logs to their lodges and dams.
- ➤ At present beavers are widely distributed through North America.

- Although beavers normally remain underwater for 3 or 4 minutes at a time, they are capable of holding their breath for 12-15 minutes if necessary.
- Beavers exhale in small spurts when they swim or work under water, and a large beaver is quite capable of traveling nearly ½ mile under the surface before it must surface for more air.
- Beavers are second only to humans in their ability to manipulate the environment.
- By building and maintaining dams, beavers can completely change the vegetation, animal life and other components of the aquatic areas in which they live.
- The ponds created by the dams and lodges are the beaver's first defense against predators like the lynx and wolf.
- Beaver's front teeth never stop growing so beavers must gnaw, chew, and chop almost all the time.

NATURAL DEFENSE

Nature's Defense is a powerful Patent Pending granular animal repellent that uses the strongest, most effective animal repellent ingredients found in nature today. Nature's Defense is the most powerful form of Beaver Control available today and your natural solution that is easy to use and guaranteed to work.

BEAVER TRAPPING

There are several types of beaver traps, both live traps and lethal traps and can be found locally in most farm supply stores. If the animal is caught alive, it must be relocated at least ten miles from the capture site and within a different water system.

TUBE DRAINAGE SYSTEM

It's possible to eliminate the threat of a beaver dam causing flooding by building a tube drainage system at the lake that allows the lake to drain and enlarge.

A GNAWING PROBLEM

Tree gnawing by beavers can be prevented by building a steel fence around the tree with chicken wire. You can also just wrap chicken wire around the tree. While these methods are labor intensive, the removal of the animal is more effective.

BEARS

General Information

People are coming into contact with bears more frequently than ever before. Therefore, the challenge is to learn how problems with bears can be avoided especially in residential areas that are in or near bear habitat.

Most injuries that are associated with bear/human encounters result in people feeding bears or when bears have easy access and are feeding on human sources of food. People will often feed bears indirectly by leaving trash, pet food and other tempting items in places that are easily accessible to bears.

Simply observing a bear walking through a yard is not cause for you to become alarmed. Just make sure all garbage is stored or handled properly and do not provoke the bear. Be sure and alert your neighbors in the vicinity and request that everyone follow the same procedures.

Bears will naturally investigate food odors and they are attracted to a variety of different foods and are not very fussy when they are hungry. They will eat garbage, bird seed, suet, pet foods; compost piles and even try to eat grease on barbecue grills. Bears have a very good sense of smell and once a bear receives a "reward" such as one of these foods, it may return to the same area several times even if no food is available.

Most bear problems in residential areas are usually temporary and occur in the spring and summer months, which is when bears emerge from their dens and summer foods such as berries ripen. Their natural food supplies are low and not very nutritious causing the bears to travel more in search of food. Also, the bears breeding season occurs from June to August and male bears tend to roam more in search of mates.

THE BEAR FACTS
- ✓ They eat mostly berries, nuts, grasses, carrion and insect larvae
- ✓ They have color vision and a keen sense of smell

- ✓ They are good tree climbers and swimmers
- ✓ They are very intelligent and curious
- ✓ They can run up to 35 miles per hour, faster than you can!
- ✓ They weigh an average of 125 to 600 pounds
- ✓ They can go without food for up to 7 months during hibernation in northern ranges
- ✓ They usually give birth to 2 to 3 cubs during the mother's sleep every other year
- ✓ They can live over 25 years in the wild, however, the average age in the wild is 18
- ✓ They are typically shy and easily frightened

THERE ARE ONLY 8 SPECIES OF BEARS

The eight species of bears alive today range in size from the large brown bears and polar bears, which can weigh UP TO 2200 and 1500 pounds to the smaller giant pandas and sun bears, which can weigh less than 300 pounds apiece.

1.AMERICAN BLACK BEARS

The black bear inhabits parts of North America and Mexico. Their diet consists of plant material such as leaves, buds, shoots, berries and nuts. The American black bear subspecies include the cinnamon bear, glacier bear, Mexican black bear, Kermody bear, Louisiana black bear and several others.

2.ASIAN BLACK BEARS

The Asian black bears are medium-sized bears and inhabit parts of Southeast Asia and the Russian Far East. Asian black bears are identified with a patch of yellowish-white fur on their chest and a black body. They closely resemble American black bears in body shape and behavior. Asian black bears will feed on bamboo shoots, leaves, herbs, grasses, fruits and nuts.

3.BROWN BEARS

Brown bears are the largest of all the bear species and are the largest living land carnivore.

They are widely distributed, inhabiting a range that includes the northern parts of North America, Europe and Asia. There are a number of subspecies of brown bears including the Carpathian bear, European brown bear, Gobi bear, grizzly bear, Kodiak bear and several others.

4.POLAR BEARS

Polar bears are the second largest of all bear species and inhabit a circumpolar region in the Arctic which stretches into northern Canada and Alaska. Polar bears usually live on pack ice, along shorelines and swim in open water. They feed on a diet of seals and smaller walrus.

5.GIANT PANDAS

 Giant pandas are relatively small bears that feed almost exclusively on bamboo shoots and leaves. They have a distinct panda bear color pattern, which is a black body, white face, black ears and black eye spots. Giant pandas are only native to the central and southern parts of western China.

6.SLOTH BEARS

Sloth bears are medium-sized bears that inhabit grasslands, forests and scrublands in Southeast Asia. They have long, shaggy fur and a white chest mark. They feed on termites, which they find using their acute sense of smell.

7.SPECTACLED BEARS

Spectacled bears are the only bear species that lives in South America. They inhabit cloud forests at elevations between 3300 to 8900 feet and also inhabit coastal deserts and high elevation grasslands, but the encroachment of humans into those habitats has restricted their range.

8.SUN BEARS

Sun bears are the smallest species of bear and inhabit lowland tropical forest in Southeast Asia. They have the shortest fur of all the bear species and are have a light, reddish-brown U-shaped patch of fur on their chest.

Fun Facts About Bears

The earliest known true bear is *Ursavus elemensis*, also known as the dawn bear and was a small, dog-sized bear that inhabited subtropical forests in Europe during the Miocene era. The dawn bear is believed to be the ancestor of all eight living bear species.

Six of the eight species of bears are classified as vulnerable or threatened with extinction with the giant panda the most threatened of all bear species, with only 1600 remaining individuals.

The koala is not a bear; it is a marsupial and is occasionally referred to as a 'koala bear', a common name it earned due to its slight resemblance to a teddy bear and lives in Australia.

SOLVING THE PROBLEM

- Store garbage inside buildings or other areas that bears cannot get to.
- Never feed bears under any circumstances.
- If your area is served by a garbage collection service, place garbage out only during the day of collection.
- Never leave even a garbage can out overnight for a morning poick up.
- Never leave pet food outside overnight.
- If bird feeders have been visited by a bear, best to stop feeding birds for 1 to 2 weeks.
- Persons living in bear roaming areas should install "bear-proof" containers or use dumpsters with heavy gauge metal lids as a solution to bear problems
- Make sure dumpsters are bolted and locked and chain down heavy metal garbage cans and secure the lids.
- Wood or plastic dumpster lids never keep bears out.

- ➢ Make sure sliding side doors can be latched so only humans can open them.
- ➢ Fencing around dumpsters or garbage collection areas can be very effective. A chain link fence with a barbwire overhang works very well.

PUT A MASK ON FOOD
If you can mask the odor of food it may keep the bears away. Sprinkling ammonia or other strong disinfectants on garbage cans have been known to be very effective.

TEACH YOUR SPOUSE TO SCREAM
Screaming, shouting, clapping your hands, blasting a car horn or motion sensitive lights may scare off a bear temporarily.

BOBCAT

General Information

Bobcat numbers are declining because of human encroachment reducing their natural habitat. Bobcat populations throughout the United States have fluctuated over the years; however, their numbers are remaining strong.
Bobcats are the most abundant wild cat in North America; they presently number anywhere from 725,000 to 1,020,000 and are active in a range from Northern Mexico to Southern Canada.

They prefer to live and hide around rocky crags and under dense bushes. Bobcats are comfortable in various habitats and are especially at home in forests, mountainous areas, semi-deserts, even brush land. Bobcats have short ear tufts and their name is related to their small, bobbed tails, which have a solid black ring around the end.

Bobcats tend to "jump" when they run much like rabbits and although they weigh in at only 16-28 pounds for males and 10-18 for females, they can be tenacious when they are hissing and spitting. Their enemies are man and disease; otherwise bobcats have very little in the way of natural enemies.

Bobcats are for the most part nocturnal mammals, however, during the winter they are also active during the day to hunt enough food to keep them alive. Males are very active and may travel several miles in a night.

They may have several dens; one main den and several others in a 5 square mile territory. They are very secretive animals and people don't get a chance to watch very often.

Bobcats are excellent stalkers and hunters and capture their prey in one great leap, using the element of surprise to catch their prey, which is usually a rabbit. However, if they will also eat squirrels, rats, mice, shrews, small deer, bats and marmots.

BOBCAT FACTS

➢ In spite of their size, bobcats are one of the most successful predators in North America because of their adaptability and variety of prey.
➢ Bobcats can take down prey animals that are at least eight times their own weight. They often kill deer and sheep in parts of their range.
➢ Bobcats will sneak up to the prey before employing their long powerful hind legs to generate great bursts of speed up to about 32 miles per hour.
➢ Bobcats are very graceful yet fierce predators and are known in Native American folklore for their courage.
➢ Bobcats belong to the Lynx genus of felines and are the smallest of the species.
➢ Today's Bobcats seem to have evolved around twenty thousand years ago from the Eurasian Lynx.
➢ Bobcats are very adaptable and are seen in a variety of habitats all across the United States, even some urban neighborhoods.
➢ Their population in Canada is limited where they are replaced by their larger relative, the Canadian Lynx.

➢ Bobcats are at least twice as large as domestic cats and may reach a length of around four feet, including their short tail.

> Even though they were hunted excessively for sport and fur trade the Bobcats have managed to survive in fairly large numbers throughout United States.

WATCH YOUR SMALL PETS
Bobcats are usually not a threat to humans; however, they may prey on small pets including cats and small dogs. Never leave your pet outside, even in your backyard if you have seen a bobcat in your neighborhood.

DETER A BOBCAT
To stop a bobcat immediately, make loud noises by banging on pots, clapping your hands or shouting. Spraying it with a garden hose works great! If the bobcat has become confined, open a gate and have everyone leave the area and it will leave on its own. If it remains, it will have to be trapped.

BOBCAT WILL NOT LEAVE
If a bobcat remains around your property for more than a few days, it may have a litter and you might want to check for kittens. If kittens are there, consider putting up with the situation for a few weeks until kittens are large enough to leave the area with their mother. If you find only kittens and no mother, be sure and leave the kittens alone and watch them from a distance since the mother is probably out looking for food. Do not feed bobcats as this can encourage them to become too comfortable around humans. Removal by animal control should be a last resort.

CHICKENS

General Information

History of the domesticated chicken goes as far back as 7000 BC and originated from India and East Asia. The chicken can probably trace its origins back as far as the dinosaurs. Chickens were carried to many areas by Polynesian seafarers and actually reached Easter Island in the 12th century CE (common era), where they were the only domesticated animals, except for the Polynesian Rat.

Their coops were built from stone and they traveled as cargo on trading ships to reach the Asian continent by way of the islands of Indonesia and from there were sent west to Europe and western Asia.

The Leghorn (no relation to Foghorn Leghorn), breed of chickens are well known for their excellent egg production. The breed was named after the Ligurian Sea, over whose waters the birds were shipped. The word Ligurian was commonly mispronounced by people not familiar with the term and eventually the birds were called Leghorns.

The first leghorn chicken appeared in the United States around 1835and later some were exported to England. Their excellent egg laying abilities made them the most utilized breed of chicken in the world. Leghorn roosters can sometimes grow as big as six pounds. While the hens will usually average around 4½ pounds. Leghorn hens are unique in the fact that their comb always flops to one side of their head.

They are very vocal and active birds and excellent foragers. Leghorns are very good at converting feed to energy and are capable of being completely self-sufficient.

CHICKEN FACTS
- A chickens' body temperature usually runs at 102-103 degrees F.
- Roosters takes 18-20 breaths a minute, a hen takes 30-35 breaths per minute.
- There are over 150 varieties of domesticated chickens.
- Chickens are not capable of sustained flight, even though they try.
- It takes a hen 24-26 hours to lay one egg.
- Chickens lay different colored eggs, from white, to brown, to green, to pink, to blue depending on the type of feed they are given.
- Chickens sold in grocery stores are 5-8 weeks old.
- A chick takes 21 days to hatch.
- Chickens were domesticated about 7000 years ago.
- Americans consume over 8 billion chickens a year.
- All domestic chickens can be genetically traced to the Red Jungle Fowl.
- It takes 4+ pounds of chicken feed to make 1 dozen eggs.

- Certain breeds were developed to provide plumage for ceremonial costumes.
- In 1925, hens laid an average of 100 eggs a year. However, in 1979, the World Record was set by a White Leghorn who laid 371 eggs in 364 days, poor chicken!
- A hen lives an average of 5-7 years, however, they have been known to up to 20 years. A hen will lay eggs her entire life, with production decreasing every year from year one.
- An egg starts begin growing into a chick when it reaches a temperature of 86 degrees F.
- There are more chickens live on Earth than people.
- Chickens can run as fast as 9 miles an hour.

The chicken capital of the world is Gainesville, Georgia. It is illegal there to eat chicken with a fork and people have been arrested for committing the crime.

- A hen lays an average of 300 eggs every year.
- A hen must turn her egg about 50 times every day. This must be done so that the yoke inside does not get stuck to the inside of the shell.

A LITTLE SQUIRT WILL DO YA

If you want to get rid of chickens, just give them a little squirt with a garden hose. Chickens hate to be squirted and will remember your property and never come back. However, it may take 2-3 times before they get the idea. Also, yell and scream, flail your arms and generate the impression that you're to be feared.

MOTION SENSOR SPRINKLERS

If you can afford it, motion sensor sprinklers will completely solve your problem, whether you're home or not or consider sending the kids out with an arsenal of BIG squirt guns.

CHICKENS HATE CHICKEN WIRE

Try cutting strips of chicken wire to cover unplanted areas of your flower beds then cover the wire with attractive mulch. You can also cover seeded beds the same way.

The seedlings will grow right up and through the wire. The chickens will dig through the mulch, but will not be very happy when they hit the wire. They can't scratch and dig through the wire, so they will eventually look elsewhere for easier pickings.

MAKE PLANT CAGES
Make individual cages that will surround specimen plants that chickens may be picking at or eating. Just form a cylinder from a length of 4-foot wire then encircle the plant with the cage. It is easy to cut a round piece from the wire to make a cover as well. From a few feet away, the chicken wire is almost invisible until they get up to it then they get frustrated and leave.

FENCE THEM OFF
You will need to prepare a number of 2-foot long sticks. Insert 4-6 inches of each stick into the soil at about a 60^0 angle and be sure they are pointing outward. You will need to space them 1-2 inches apart all the way around your flower bed. If you do this right, you can create an effective barrier that actually looks like a cute rustic fence.

BEGONE, CHICKENS & BIRDS
Try covering susceptible flower beds with bird netting, which is tough and also weather resistant. Bird netting is a great way to keep wild birds out of your berry bushes as well as the chickens.

ZAPPPPPPPPP
Run a couple of strands of electric wire around your flower bed or vegetable garden. One wire should be about 5 inches off the ground, the other about 12 inches above the ground. Most garden and farm supply centers can advise you how to properly install this very simple and inexpensive control measure. It usually, only takes getting zapped once or twice for even the dumbest chicken to get the picture. It's also an excellent deterrent for just about any other type of animal pest.

COUGARS (PUMA)

General Information
Because of its presence in so many regions, cougar has earned more names, than any other animal.

They have been called mountain lion, mountain screamer, puma, catamount, Florida panther, American lion and many others.
They are a large graceful cat that is exceeded in size only by the jaguar among cats. The name puma is derived from usage by the Inca Indians.

The cougar ranges from the southern third of British Columbia to Patagonia in habitats such mountains, deserts and jungles, but because of hunting by humans, it is now generally restricted to wilderness areas. The cougar is found over a wider range than any other mammal in the western hemisphere, except for man. Once common, the cougar has been eradicated in many areas, and its survival is now threatened.

The Eastern cougar or puma of North America and the Florida cougar (panther) of the Southern United States are considered endangered. A male puma may grow to be 6 feet long with a tail of 2-3 feet. Cougars' long tails may actually be one-third of their total body length. An adult male cougar weighs between 140-200 pounds and a female cougar, between 90-120 pounds. Their coat ranges in color from reddish to brownish yellow or gray.

Pumas usually live to about 12 years old, but have been known to live up to 19 years in captivity. Cougars are the most active at dusk and dawn. However, they will roam and hunt any time of the day or night and in all seasons. Cougars will eat a variety of food, but rely on deer where available. It will also eat wild sheep, elk, dogs, cats, rabbits, beaver, raccoons, grouse, and occasionally livestock.

Cougars are capable of killing a 600 pound moose or full size elk. It is an excellent climber and jumper, and often jumps from limbs onto its prey. It has powerful limbs allowing it to jump to heights of 18 feet or more.

COUGAR FACTS
  ➤ Despite its heavy build; cougars look like smaller felines in its physical makeup and is often not included in big cat categories owing to its inability to roar.
  ➤ With its rudder-like tail and bodily structure, cougars are often said to be related to the cheetah in its evolution.

- Cougars are excellent athletes using their long hind legs to give them an incredible horizontal leaping ability of almost forty feet in one bound, which is second only to the snow leopard which can bound forty five feet in a jump.
- Cougars use their great speed and momentum to take down their prey then proceed to make the kill with a lethal neck bite.
- If they are unable to finish their meal in one sitting, they will usually save their kill under leaves and shrubs and return to it later.
- Despite being a prolific hunter, cougars are not at the top of food chain in many of their ecosystems and face stiff competition at the hands of bears, wolves and jaguars.

TRAPPING IS THE ONLY HUMANE METHOD AND SHOULD BE DONE BY APROFESSIONAL.

COYOTE

General Information

The Coyote is actually a small wolf and is native to western North America. It is a carnivorous animal and similar to a collie. Its voice is a snapping bark that is followed by a prolonged, shrill howl, similar to a wolf. Coyotes are also known as the American jackal or the prairie wolf. Coyotes are presently found in Canada, North America and Central America.

Coyotes hunt in packs of 2-3 and often sleep in holes in the ground. They only have just one mate for life. They weight 15 to 46 pounds and are about 40 inches long. Their habitat is forests, plains deserts and mountain regions. They have a lifespan of about 15 years, similar to a dog, however they can run up to 43 MPH.

They are carnivorous scavengers and will eat your small pets if they can catch one. They have numerous survival skills and are a very intelligent animal. One of the coyote facts and the most important is its smell. It uses it to find food as well as to avoid other predators. Coyotes are mostly active during the early morning and at twilight.

Coyotes will communicate with each other in a very unusual way with a high pitched scream and howls are the most common, but they also bark, growl, wail, and even squeal sometimes. When a lot of coyotes meet they scream as if performing some weird ritual.

COYOTE FACTS

➤ Coyotes will sometimes walk on toes to avoid other predators, It is one of the amazing coyote facts and look a bit strange when you see them tip toing around.

➤ Coyotes mark their territory by peeing just like dogs. Urine marking is used by many animals.

➤ Coyotes use holes or a borrowed burrow for sleeping as well as when giving birth.

➤ Coyotes hunt in groups of 3 or 4 and rarely hunt alone.

➤ Their diet consists of all kinds of animals such as rabbits, insects, mice and small animals.

➤ Coyotes are able to detect hunters coming from a mile away.

➤ The main enemy of coyotes, are bears, wolves and other coyotes as well as humans, however, they are able to escape their enemies because of their speed and swimming abilities.

➤ As an aggressive gesture, the coyote's tail becomes bushier and turns sideways.

➤ A coyote's sense of hearing is good enough to be used for finding food and avoiding predators.

➤ Coyotes will hold its head low and tuck its tail between the legs, just like a dog when scared.

➤ Coyote will usually supply live mice to their pups, for hunting practice.

 ➤ Movement and position of a coyote's ears communicate its mood and rank.

➤ Coyotes select a mate when they are about 2 years old and remain with him/her throughout their life.

➤ Coyotes are clever enough to trick most other animals and even birds.

TRAPS ARE THE ONLY ANSWER

Since we do not recommend shooting them, the only other method is to hire a professional to trap them, which is expensive! If they don't have a food source they will leave your area. The food source includes your pets!

CROCODILE

General Information

Crocodiles are carnivorous and have very strong jaws that can crack a turtle shell. They also eat fish, snails and other invertebrates, birds, frogs, and mammals that come to close when they are hungry. They have very sharp teeth and use them to seize and hold prey; however, small prey is swallowed whole. If the prey is very large, crocodilians shake it apart into smaller, manageable pieces.

If the prey is very large, crocodiles bite it then spin on the long axis of their bodies to tear the prey apart, making it easier to eat.

One of the easiest ways to distinguish an alligator from a crocodile is by looking at the teeth; however, this may be a bit dangerous since if they open wide, you may end up in it. The large fourth tooth in the lower jaw of an alligator fits into a socket in the upper jaw but is not visible when the mouth is closed. This does not occur in crocodiles. Alligators have between 74 and 80 teeth in their mouth at any one time. As their teeth wear down they are replaced and an alligator can go through 2,000 to 3,000 teeth in a lifetime.

CROCODILE FACTS

➢ The largest crocodile species is the saltwater crocodile and is found from India to northern Australia and Fiji. It can reach a length of 23 feet in length and 1,000 pounds in weight.
➢ A crocodile egg is no larger than that of a goose egg.
➢ The smallest crocodile is the dwarf crocodile from central Africa, which has a maximum length of 6½ feet.
➢ Crocodile skin is considered one of the finest and best, being soft and durable for making shoes and bags.
➢ In many tribal societies the skin of a crocodile is used as a symbol of high status, however, only the skin on the belly has these qualities.
➢ The back skin is covered in bones (called osteoderms) that are able to reflect arrows, spears and even low caliber bullets.
➢ A crocodile skin purse can cost $15,000.

- The value of the crocodile has caused poaching and many of the species are now threatened.
- Crocodiles are very aggressive during mating season.
- Crocodiles swallow stones to grind up their food in their stomachs.
- Crocodiles are capable of exerting enormous pressure when they close their jaws, but the force required for opening them is very weak and a rubber band can be used to keep the jaws shut.
- Crocodiles may be seen on the river banks with their jaws wide open, which is their method of keeping cool since they sweat through their mouth.
- About 99% of crocodiles, offspring are eaten during their first year of life by large monitor lizards, herons and even alligators.
- Crocodiles have a powerful tail, which helps them swim around 25 miles an hour and they can stand underwater for 2-3hours.
- Crocodiles can live up to 70 years.
- Crocodiles have vertical pupils, which can open wide and allow them to see in the dark.
- A mother crocodile carries her young in a pouch inside her mouth.
- In order to dive deeper, crocodiles have been known to swallow stones.
- Crocodiles can consume their prey under water as well as above water since their throats have the ability to not swallow water while they eat underwater.
- Crocodiles are able to keep their eyes open under water.
- Crocodiles close their nostrils while under water.

NOT A GOOD PET!
The only way to get rid of a crocodile is to call a professional and have them trap and remove it.

FERAL CATS

General Information

DIFFERENCE BETWEEN A STRAY CAT AND A FERAL CAT
A feral cat is basically a wild animal that is of the same species as a domesticated house cat. There are an estimated 60 million to 120 million feral cats within the U.S. alone.

Stray cats are pet cats, which were lost or abandoned, while feral cats are the offspring of lost or abandoned pet cats or other feral cats, which are not spayed or neutered. Stray cats are still used to contact with people and are tame, but feral cats become somewhat wild and are not accustomed to contact with people and are too fearful and wild to be handled.

WHERE FEARAL CATS LIVE

Feral cats usually live in a colony with a group of related cats. The colony will occupy and defend a specific territory where food (a restaurant dumpster, person who feeds them) and shelter (underneath a porch or in an abandoned building) are available.

Since feral cats typically fear strangers, it is likely that people may not realize that feral cats are living nearby since the cats are rarely seen.

FOOD COMPETITORS

Feral cats feed extensively on songbirds, game birds, mice and other rodents, rabbits, and other wildlife. In doing so, they lower the carrying capacity of an area for native predators such as foxes, raccoons, coyotes, bobcats, weasels, and other animals that compete for the same food base.

FERAL DOGS

General Information

POPULATION EXPLOSION ON OUR STREETS

The United States has an enormous feral dog problem in most major cities. This country has literally experienced an explosion in the number of dogs that are abandoned by their owners and an increase in feral dogs that are born, live and die on the streets, never having been socialized to humans.

The epidemic is recent and only since the 1980s and caused by a lethal combination of vastly increased dog fighting, dogs bred for aggressiveness, and the reduction animal control due to lack of finances.

Los Angeles, Detroit, New Orleans, Cleveland, New York, Baltimore, Houston, Indianapolis, Santa Fe and Pittsburgh are all reporting "an epidemic of feral and abandoned dogs." 40,000 Americans now take part in dog fighting. There are an estimated 50,000 street dogs in Los Angeles. In  Los Angeles County and City 200,000 residents were bitten by abandoned dogs in one year. In New Orleans, estimates are placed at 120,000 stray dogs after hurricane Katrina

FOXES

General Information

There are five species of the fox that are found in North America: The red fox, the gray fox, the Kit Fox, the Swift fox, and the Island Fox. The two most common are the red fox and the gray fox.

Male adult foxes are known commonly as vixes. Female adult foxes are known as vixens and a group of foxes is called a skulk.

During the past several years, the reputation of the fox has improved due to its portrayals in fiction and literature. Between the red fox and the gray fox, the red fox is the larger of the two species weighing seven to fifteen pounds and growing to three feet in length and having a foot and a half long tail. Both the red and gray fox will dig their own dens or occupy the abandoned dens of woodchucks, badgers or other burrowing animals.

Their dens or burrows are used to raise their young or escape the cold weather. Both foxes prefer to rest under, brush piles or fallen logs. Foxes are dangerous to humans only when they are rabid and between the two, the gray fox is more reclusive. The red fox has been seen walking through yards and ignoring any humans that may be around.

Both foxes will dig under fences to reach outdoor pets such as rabbits, small dogs or cats and they love poultry.

They pay little attention to adult cats, because they are almost of the same size, however they will go after kittens. Red Foxes can live 10 years in captivity, but generally only live 3 years in the wild. They are found throughout the British Isles including Ireland, but absent from most other islands. They are also native to the rest of Europe and North America, Asia, North Africa and introduced to Australia and New Zealand in the mid-19th century.

The fox has been hunted by humans for thousands of years since its thick red fur has always been in demand. In fact, an increase in the popularity of fox fur in the late 1970s caused many more foxes than usual to be killed. However, since the decline in fur prices, this trade has decreased substantially.

Farmers have always considered the fox to be a pest because it will prey on poultry and sheep. However, most chickens are caged up securely so the fox rarely gets the chance to steal them. In continental Europe, foxes carry the fatal disease rabies.

FOX FACTS
- The Tibetan Fox looks more like a big-headed wolf.
- Foxes are solitary animals that do not really prefer to live in packs.
- Foxes are found in almost every kind of habitat. They also show an ability to easily adapt to the presence of humans.
- The Fennec fox is the smallest fox seen amongst all the species and this tiny animal weighs only 3½ pounds.
- Foxes use different sounds and pitches to communicate between each other. Their high-pitched sounds are especially noticeable during the mating period in the months of December to January.
- Compared to wolves, foxes are smaller in size. They are characterized by a sharp muzzle and bushy tail. Their chest and underbelly usually have a shade of white or gray.
- Physical characteristics may vary with the different species of fox. The Red fox will have a reddish brown coat and the Arctic fox has very thick fur. Characteristics depend on the habitat of the fox.
- Even though foxes belong to the Canidae family along with dogs, they also display behavior patterns that are similar to cats. The vertically slit eyes are on similar lines of the feline cats and they have retractable claws.

- Foxes generally prefer areas of higher latitudes. They can also adapt themselves well to an urban environment.
- Foxes have been used successfully on fruit farms to control rodent pests. Foxes will get rid of rodents without really harming the fruits.
- Foxes will feed on rodents, worms, insects, birds and all types of relatively smaller sized animals and store their food so that it can be consumed later on during the day.
- Foxes are basically nocturnal animals and prefer to hunt at night.

FENCES WORK GREAT

You will need to construct a net wire fence with openings of 3 inches or less to exclude red foxes. The fence needs to be buried with the bottom of the fence 1 to 2 feet with an apron of net wire extending at least 12 inches outward from the bottom. You may also need a top or roof of net wire to exclude all foxes, since some will climb a fence. Also, a 3-wire electric fence with wires spaced 6 inches, 12 inches, and 18 inches above the ground will repel red foxes. You can also use  fences that incorporate net and electric wires with excellent effectiveness.

BRIGHT FLASHING LIGHTS

Flashing lights, such as rotating beacons or strobe lights, may provide temporary protection in relatively small areas or in livestock or poultry enclosures. Try a combination of frightening devices used at irregular intervals and it should provide better protection than use of a single device because animals may have more difficulty in adapting to these disturbances.

DOGS TO THE RESCUE

When properly trained there are some breeds of dog, such as Great Pyrenees and Akbash dogs that have been useful in preventing predation on sheep. The effectiveness of dogs, even the guard dog breeds, seems to depend entirely on training and the individual disposition of the dog.

TRAPPING FOXES

Trapping is a very effective; however a great deal of expertise is required to effectively trap foxes.

Trapping by an inexperienced person may serve to educate foxes, making them very difficult to catch, even by experienced trappers. Special traps suitable for foxes are the Nos. 1½, 1¾, and 2 double coil-spring trap and the Nos. 2 and 3 double long-spring trap. Traps with offset and padded jaws cause less injury to confined animals and facilitate the release of non-target captures.

Your state and local wildlife authorities regulate the traps and sets that can be used for trapping. Consult your local agency personnel for restrictions that pertain to your area.

FINDING THEIR DEN

You can locate fox dens by observing signs of fox activity and by careful observation during the early and late hours of the day when adult foxes are moving trying to find food. Preferred den sites are usually on a low rise facing a southerly direction. When fox pups are several weeks old, they will spend time outside the den in the early morning and evening hours. They leave many signs of their presence, such as matted down vegetation and remnants of food, including bits of bone, feathers and hair. If it is a frequently used den site it will have a distinctive odor.

GEESE

General Information

Geese can live to be 20-25 years old so if your get a goose, be prepared to have it around for company for quite a while. Better be prepared to have a couple of them around for quite a while since geese like to hang around in groups and need companionship. If you don't want to breed them then you had better get females since males fight.

Geese require a large, fenced enclosure with shade areas, several water containers and including one for swimming, seed containers and a large patch of grass. They like cold weather and rain and never seek shelter from either. Geese eat scratch feed, grass and various greens, such as collard and turnip greens, spinach and kale.

Geese make excellent watchdogs since they are alert and quick to sound the alarm, very loudly, when anything out of the ordinary occurs. There are two major genera among the geese: Anser geese and Branta geese. Anser geese usually have pink, orange or gray legs and bills and their bills are serrated. Geese spend most of the day foraging for food, which is usually obtained by grazing.

Geese prefer fertilized over unfertilized grass for feeding and are attracted to golf courses, playgrounds and other well-maintained lawns.

Geese fly in V formation since the flapping of wings of one goose creates uplift for the goose immediately following. Flying in V formation also adds at least 71% greater flying range than if each goose flew alone. When the goose in front gets tired, another goose will take over the front position.

Geese will honk to encourage those up front to keep up their speed. Geese have strong affections for others in their group. If a goose gets sick or is wounded, a couple of other geese may drop out of formation to help and protect him. They will try to stay with the disabled goose until he dies or is able to fly again. They will then either fly together or join another formation to catch up with their group.

GOOSE FACTS
- ➢ Geese have a very strong instinct to return to their general area of birth to mate and nest. They will either return to the exact site or to a nearby pond or other body of water.
- ➢ Migratory geese will fly 2-3,000 miles to return to these sites. Geese will build their nests on the ground at isolated sites close to water.
- ➢ The female goose will build her nest and line it with down plucked from her body. She will then lay one egg each day until the full clutch of about 5 eggs is obtained. After all the eggs have been laid, she will sit on her nest to incubate the eggs, which takes about 30 days. Whenever she leaves the nest, she will cover the eggs with sticks to keep them warm and to camouflage to nest. During all this, the male goose will stand somewhere nearby to keep watch, but not too close as to give away the location of the nest to a predator.
- ➢ The parents will lead the goslings to the safety of open water within 24 hours of birth.

Goslings are able to dive and swim 30-40 feet underwater when they are just 1 day old and will eat almost continuously.

➢ Goslings are able to fly when they are about 2-3 months old. They will stay with their parents and follow them back the following year to the place where they were born. There they will learn to form, flocks with other young geese. Geese are one of the few birds in which the family does not break up at the end of the breeding season.

➢ Once a year, adult geese will lose flight and tail feathers, which is called molting. They are unable to fly until the new feathers have come in. This takes about 6 weeks. Geese like to be near water during the molting season, to be able to escape from predators.

➢ The natural predators of geese are foxes, owls, raccoons and snapping turtles.

➢ When geese are scared or threatened, they will stretch out their necks and honk loudly. Male geese are very protective of their female partner and will often stand between her and a perceived threat.

➢ Geese use about 10 different sounds to communicate, depending on the situation confronting them.

BAD TASTING GRASS

A product called, Flight Control™, is mixed with water and sprayed on a lawn. Once applied, it affects the way ultraviolet light is reflected, making the lawn appear unappetizing to geese. If that doesn't stop them and they eat anyway, it may taste okay but it causes intestinal irritation. It won't hurt them, but after two or three days, geese get the message and forage elsewhere.

PLASTIC LINE KEEPS THEM AWAY

The Goose Grid™ is a black non-reflective plastic line that is installed around a pond. You install three lines: one at 6 inches, another at 12 and another at 18 inches. The geese can still fly over the line to get into the pond, but they quickly tire of running into a virtually invisible barrier as they waddle out for lunch.

IT FLASHES BEFORE THEIR EYES

An excellent goose deterrent is made by awaywithgeese.com in Cincinnati. Geese like to sleep on water to stay safe from predators; however, this product makes it impossible for the geese to get a good night's sleep. The product has a light attached to a flotation device; the light flashes every two seconds and keeps them awake. After three or four sleepless nights, they look for a better spot. The light uses solar power!

BETTER THAN A RUBBER DUCKY

This works great! Purchase some rubber geese and place them in your pond on their sides. The geese see this and think the pond Is not safe, see dead deer, and will bypass it. Geese will instinctively avoid water if they think it is unsafe.

THE EYE IS WATCHING!

You can purchase a motion detector that works with your sprinkler system and when the geese come around it will set off the sprinklers scaring them away.

SWAN POND/LAKE

Mute Swans will defend their young quite aggressively, and this is a danger most incoming geese will try to avoid. Swan decoys in your lawn, ponds, or near your lakeshore property can be placed out when you know the migratory season for geese has begun.

TALL GRASSES WORK GREAT!

Allow tall grasses around a pond or lake to grow at least 18 inches high in a band roughly ten feet wide around shorelines to help make your property less attractive to geese. Geese like to be kept abreast of the activities of nearby animals, particularly predators. They will be less likely to make your property into a nesting ground if they don't have an adequate visual field to ensure their safety.

GOATS

General Information

Goats were one of the first domesticated animal; about 10,000 years ago in the Zagros Mountains of Iran.

Ancient nomadic tribes began to keep them for easy access to milk, hair, meat and skins. The domesticated goats were generally kept in herds that wandered on hills or other grazing areas, often tended by goat herders who were frequently children or adolescents, similar to the more widely known shepherd herders. These methods of herding are still used today in many parts of the world.

Historically, goat hides were used for water and to carry wine when traveling and transporting wine for personal use and for sale. The hides were also been used to produce parchment, which was the most common material used for writing in Europe until the invention of the printing press.

Goats are ruminants and have a four-chambered stomach consisting of the rumen, reticulum, omasum and the abomasum. Goats have horizontal slit-shaped pupils, which increases peripheral depth perception.

In some climates, goats are able to breed anytime of the year. However, in temperate climates and among the Swiss breed of goats, the breeding season starts as the day length shortens and ends in early spring.

Freshening (coming into milk production) starts at kidding and milk production varies with the breed, age and diet of the doe. On average, a good quality dairy doe will give at least 6 pounds of milk per day.

According to some literature, goats are supposed to be willing to eat almost anything. The digestive systems of a goat, does allow nearly any organic substance to be broken down and used as nutrients.
Contrary to the goat's reputation, they are quite fussy in their habits, and like the tips of woody shrubs and trees, as well as an occasional broad leaved plant. Goats do not usually consume garbage, tin cans or clothing.

A goat is very useful to humans both alive and dead, first as a renewable provider of milk and then as meat and hide. The intestine of a goat is used to make "catgut", which is still in use as a material for internal human sutures. Goat milk contains less lactose than cow's milk, so is less likely to trigger lactose intolerance. The milk is naturally homogenized since it lacks the protein agglutinin.

Goat butter is white because the goats produce milk with the yellow beta-carotene (pre-cursor to vitamin A) converted to a colorless form of vitamin A. Goat cheese is known as chèvre in France, after the French word for "goat". Feta is a well-known Greek variety that may be made with a blend of goat and sheep milk.

GOAT FACTS
- Goats were the first animals to be used for milk by humans.
- There are over 210 breeds of goats worldwide.
- Goats were first brought to America by Columbus in 1492.
- Goats were regularly imported into America around 1912.
- The female goat is called a "doe" or "nanny."
- The male goat is called a "buck" or "billy."
- A baby goat is called a "kid."
- Goats do not have teeth in their upper front jaw.
- Goats have 24 molars and 8 incisors.
- Both male and female goats can have beards.

- Normally goats have two teats and cows have four.
- Goats prefer browse over grass and grass to clover.
- Goats live 8 to 12 years.
- Goat size is extremely variable depending on the breed. Females can range from 22 to 300 pounds with males ranging larger at 27 to 380 pounds. Meat breeds are generally heavier than dairy breeds.
- Both male and female goats can have horns and beards. Male goats can breed as early as 4 months old, and females at 7 months old.
- There are approximately 500 million goats in the world. The U.S. has approximately 3 million with Texas leading production. China has 170 million.
- Throughout the world, it is estimated that more people eat goat meat and drink goat milk than any other animal.
- It is estimated that 72% of the world's milk consumption is from goats.
- Goat milk is fairly similar in nutrients to cow's milk and can replace it in virtually any recipe. However, goat milk is "naturally" homogenized. The fat molecules are five times smaller than in cow's milk which makes it much easier for humans to digest.

- Goats are sometimes kept with racehorses as a companion animal. This is thought to have a calming effect on the horse.
- Goats are good swimmers.
- It is rumored that goats "discovered" coffee when ancient goat herders noticed that goats had more energy after eating the beans of the coffee plant.
- Mohair comes from the Angora goat and each goat can produce about 4 pounds of fleece per year.
- Cashmere comes from the Cashmere goat and each Cashmere goat can produce about one pound of fleece per year.
- Goats are hollow-horned, bearded, ruminant mammals. They are raised for wool, milk and meat in the U.S. Goats are also used to make gelatin.
- 37. Goats don't like to get wet and prefer to seek shelter when it is raining.
- Goats are quite agile creatures and in some cases they can jump over 5 feet.
- Azalea bushes are poisonous to goats.
- Goat's milk is higher in calcium, vitamin A and niacin than cow's milk.
- Goat meat is lower in fat and cholesterol compared to beef, pork, mutton and even poultry.
- Goats; are one the cleanliest animals and is much more selective feeders than cows, sheep, pigs, swine and even dogs.
- Approximately 1.5 million pounds of goat meat is imported into the U.S. every week from Australia and New Zealand because domestic production and processing systems in this country cannot keep pace with the demand.

HEDGEHOGS

General Information

There are 17 species of hedgehog found through parts of Europe, Asia and Africa and New Zealand. There are no hedgehogs native to Australia and no living species native to North America. Hedgehogs share distant ancestry with shrews and have changed little over the last 15 million years. Like many of the first mammals on earth they have adapted to a nocturnal, insectivorous way of life.

A defense that all species of hedgehogs have is the ability to roll into a tight ball, causing all of the spines to point outwards. However, how effective it really is depends on the number of spines and they are more likely to try to run away and sometimes even attack the intruder.

Hedgehogs are basically small spine covered mammals weighing less than 1.3 pounds eats insects and prefers to live alone. They are primarily nocturnal, which means that they are most active at night. The wild hedgehogs are native to Europe, Asia, and Africa. Even though they resemble porcupine, keep in mind that these animals are completely different. Hedgehog spines do not detach and don't have barbs and are only used primarily as a defensive mechanism when the animal rolls into a ball.

Hedgehogs are known for their spines, however, the spines actually evolved from hair as a natural defensive mechanism. Each spine is hollow and made stiff by keratin. Hedgehogs are never born with a full set of quills but grow them in a process called quilling, where every few months the baby spines fall out and are replaced by new spines.

Quilling usually begins at four months and continues again every two weeks or so for about three months to a full year, however, some hedgehogs will just quill; at their own pace. Hedgehog temperature requirement is 73-76^{0}F. If hedgehogs are not kept within a specific temperature range, they will attempt to go into hibernation.

When living in the wild, hedgehogs normally hibernate throughout the winter months when temperatures are cold. Pet hedgehogs cannot hibernate safely and must be kept at a safe temperature or they will waste away and die. If a hedgehog becomes very lazy, wobbly and is cool to the touch, they may be trying to hibernate and the cage temperature is too low

HEDGEHOG FACTS
➢ Most pet hedgehogs will live between four to six years.
➢ Hedgehogs will reach maturity in a little less than one year.
➢ Females can begin to reproduce at two to three months.
➢ Males as early as a month and a half old.

- Hedgehog litters are anywhere from a couple babies to as many as nine. The average size is typically about four.
- Hedgehogs as pets eat insects, cooked lean meats, fruits, veggies and commercial high quality cat food with few additives.
- If you notice small pink dots on your hands after handling your pet hedgehog, you're most likely not allergic.
- Quills of your spiny hedgehog have just caused a lot of tiny puncture marks on your skin.
- Be sure and wash your hands before and after handling your hedgehog to prevent infection.
- Hedgehogs have a degree of natural immunity towards snake venom thanks to a protein, called erinacin, which is present in their muscular system.
- The hedgehog quills are different from the porcupine since quills from a hedgehog cannot be easily removed from the animal.
- Hedgehogs have relatively poor eye sight, a fact which should be taken into account when caring for and interacting with hedgehogs.
- Hedgehogs of today are amazingly similar to the ones who roamed the planet 15 million years ago.
- Hedgehogs are considered to be insectivores, relying on insects for much of their dietary needs. They are, however, opportunistic feeders who will eat almost anything they find.
- When necessary, a hedgehog can run over six feet per second. In fact, many hedgehogs will attempt to escape an attacker before they roll into a protective, spiny ball.
- Hedgehogs have very sensitive senses of smell and hearing. They can even hear in the ultrasonic range.
- Hedgehogs prefer controlled periods of light and darkness, as well as undisturbed periods of rest.

PUT UP WITH THEM OR TRAP THEM

Since hedgehogs are good for the garden, consuming bugs they are usually not a pest, however, if they do bother you the only way to get rid of the humanely is to trap them and release them 10 miles away.

HOT SAUCE SPRAY

If you want to keep them out of your garden then just prepare a spray with 1 part of hot sauce and 5 parts of water then spray the area. You will never see them again.

IGUANAS

General Information

The green iguanas are one of the largest lizards in the United States and average around 6.5 feet long and weigh in at about 11 pounds. They are also one of the most popular reptile pets in the United States, even though they are somewhat difficult to care for properly. In captivity, iguanas usually die within the first year and many are (because of the difficulty caring for them) are either turned loose by their owners or given to reptile rescue groups.

The green iguanas are found in the rain forests of northern Mexico, Central America, North America, the Caribbean Islands and southern Brazil. They spend most of their lives in the canopy and in Florida's shorelines. When they live in the canopy they descend only infrequently to mate, lay eggs, or change trees.

They are primarily herbivores and are active during the day, feeding on leaves, flowers, and fruit. They generally live in the vicinity of water and are excellent swimmers. When threatened, they will leap from a branch, often from great heights to escape jump into the water below. They are also tough enough to land on solid ground from a height of 40 feet and survive.

Iguanas are fast and agile on land and they have strong jaws with razor-sharp teeth and sharp tails, which make up half their body length and can be used as whips to drive off predators. They can also detach their tails if caught and will grow another without permanent damage.

The average life span in the wild is 20 years and it is much shorter in captivity since many owners do not have the appropriate knowledge to take care of iguanas.

IGUANA FACTS

- Iguanas can stay under water for 28 minutes.
- Mother never meets baby: iguana mothers lay the eggs underground and leave them. Babies hatch, dig themselves out, and are on their own to survive.
- If an iguana's tail is cut off, they can grow another one.
- Green Iguanas can reach 5 to 6 feet in length and weigh up to 18 pounds. There is a reason that many are calling them "Giant Green Iguanas."
- Green Iguanas will need a portion of a room or an entire room when they reach adulthood. Keeping a 5 foot lizard in a fish tank of any size is impossible.
- Adult male Green Iguanas most can become aggressive for 3 months out of the year when it is breeding season.
- Adult female Green Iguanas are highly likely to produce eggs even without a male present during breeding season every year. Without proper care they can die from this.
- Iguanas must be housed in cages which are at least 6 feet high and 12 feet wide and deep. The cages must be equipped with ultra violet light facility and a temperature of 70 - 80ºC that helps them in digesting food.
- Iguanas are herbivores and hence should be fed a vegetarian diet only.
- They also draw water out of the food they eat, and hence can be fed with green beans, melons and strawberries. No animal protein supplements must be given.
- Like all animals, iguanas also show signs of aggression during mating season. During this period, they should be left along with their female partners until the mating season gets over.
- Stuffed toys are also put inside the cages for iguanas to play. They are social animals after all and like to nibble and chew whatever comes their way.
- On trees and shrubs, a slick metal collar of 6 to 12 inches can be placed around the trunk of the plant to keep iguanas from climbing the plant and eating the flowers.

TRAPPING THEM!

You can try trapping or snaring iguanas. The best place to put traps or snares is at the end of recently erected fences.

The iguana will walk along the fence and right into the traps as it looks for a way around the new fence.

PEST-RID TO THE RESCUE
There is an all-natural product that comes in both a spray and granules that will repel iguanas. It repels by odor and taste and will not harm the animals.

GETTING RID OF AN IGUANA
If you call in a wildlife trapper to remove an iguana, another will soon take its place. It is more effective to make your yard iguana resistant. There are a number of steps you can take to iguana-proof your yard:

1. Install caged screen enclosures to protect your pool and yard.
2. Install electric fencing around your yard, seawall and docks.
3. Use sheet metal guards on trees and dock pilings to keep iguanas from climbing.
4. Keep iguanas off your boat by tying plastic bottles on the lines.
5. Protect your pool deck with childproof fencing.
6. Use wire mesh screening to protect garden plants.
7. Remove fruit trees (except citrus, which they do not eat) and flowering plants from your yard.
8. Remove dense thickets, piles of landscape timber and rocks.
9. Trim bushes and trees away from your house, pool, seawall and dock.
10. Fill vacant burrows with cement and sand.
11. Spray a protective border around your yard or plants using neem oil or garlic spray. Iguanas do not like the smell and taste of these nontoxic biopesticides.

MINK

General Information

Mink have dark brown fur and a long tail that becomes progressively darker towards the tip as well as have white patches on their chest and throat. Their average weight is 3-5 pounds and they have elongated slender bodies with short, stocky legs. The females are slightly smaller than males.

Males grow to be about two feet long. Their burrow, holes in streams and riverbanks have a four-inch diameter opening are an indication that mink are present. Mink have 34 teeth and can emit a strong musky odor with their scent glands similar to skunks, but the distance the odor can be detected is more limited.

Mink are most active at night, early dawn and late dusk and excellent swimmers, spending most of their time hunting in ponds, streams and other wetland areas. They have oily guard hairs that waterproof and protect their coats. Predators normally shy away and foxes, bobcats, great horned owls and alligators are not a serious threat to mink populations since mink may hiss, snarl, screech and excrete an odorous fluid from their scent glands when threatened.

Mating season for mink is around January and March with an average of 3-4 young mink, called kits, usually born in late April or May. Adult females can have one litter, ranging from 1-8 kits every year.

Minks are carnivores and opportunistic feeders, meaning they will readily consume a large variety of both aquatic and land prey, based on availability. They will eat fish, insects, frogs, snails, rats, mice, squirrels, chipmunks, rabbits, snakes, young snapping turtles, waterfowl and other birds, bird eggs and in saltwater areas even crabs.

Mink are found in almost all 49 continental states, although they may be extremely sparse or absent in dryer states such as CA, NV, UT, NM, west TX and all of AZ.

They prefer water sources and wetland areas such as rivers, streams, creeks, beaver ponds, lakes and saltwater and freshwater marshes.

Mink are able to dig their own burrows, but they prefer to use ready-made den sites such as burrows under tree roots, bridge crossings, rock piles, ditches, crevices, as well as abandoned beaver dams and holes in streams and river banks.

MINK FACTS
➢ Mink are usually shy and avoid humans, however, at times will exhibit boldness when they become curious.

- Although mink are sometimes found traveling or living far from water, most prefer the habitats found along the shores of streams and ponds.
- Mink usually hug the shores as they travel, and prefer staying on dry land when they have a choice. Obstacles such as a protruding rock or log may cause the mink to detour into the water.
- Mink are preyed upon mainly by fox, coyotes, bobcats and dogs.
- Internal parasites include flukes, roundworms, and tapeworms are commonly found in mink including parasites such as fleas, ticks and lice.
- Mink are vulnerable to distemper, encephalitis, and rabies.
- At 7 years of age a mink is considered old and worn teeth are an indication of age.

FENCES WILL WORK
It would be best to build a fence around your property to keep minks from getting to your chickens or other animals. If you are going to build a fence, it would be best to fence with galvanized sheeting and gauge wire to keep minks out. Build a fence that is at least five feet tall and to further keep minks out of your property, put rags containing dog or cat urine on or near your fence. You should also place poultry netting around chicken coups to further protect your property from minks.

TRAPPING IS A GOOD SOLUTION
You will need to use body-grip, double-door or leg-hold traps on or near your property to capture minks if you are unsuccessful in keeping them off your property with fencing.

Place the traps near mink dens, which are usually narrow holes or spaces also mink often live in other animals' holes, such as burrows by muskrats or beavers or in fallen logs. Since the animals tend to find new homes frequently this makes them hard to catch.

After you catch them, move the minks to another location or take them to an animal control agency.

FROGS TO THE RESCUE
Dig a hole for a trap and put food, such as fish or frogs into the trap to capture minks if your other trapping methods don't work.

Be sure and place the hole in a riverbank and fill it with a minimal amount of water to have a better chance to catching minks. After you catch one or more mink, use a cage to move them.

HIRE A PROFESSIONAL
Either hire a professional or call an animal control agency to help you to get rid of minks, especially if you have no experience dealing with this type of pest. While it will cost you money to get a professional, you will not have to deal with traps.

PIPE TRAPS ARE EFFECTIVE
A very successful method of trapping is to dig a piece of round drain pipe into the river bank side above the water level then cover the pipe leaving the end open to the river, put the set trap inside the pipe. Place the bait inside it to catch the first mink. Once you have caught one mink in the trap there is no longer a need to bait the trap, this is because the mink will smell that another mink has been in the trap and then enter as they are a very inquisitive animal. Sometimes they will just enter the trap in the pipe as cover from strong rain and cold, weather.

MUSKRAT

General Information
Muskrats are mammals and are warm blooded. They give birth to their

young and are related to the mainly aquatic North American rodent. It is the largest member of the rat and mouse rodent family. Muskrats live in freshwater and saltwater marshes, lakes, ponds, and streams. They often build dome-shaped houses in marshes. These houses are made up of plants, which protect the muskrat from predators, since the only entrance is underwater.

Some muskrats live in burrows on the water banks and hibernate during the cold winter months in their lodges. Muskrats are about 12 inches long and weigh roughly 2 to 4 pounds. Muskrats eat water plants and shellfish and are covered with thick, insulating brown fur. The color of the fur ranges from dark brown on the head and back to a light greyish-brown on the belly. The coat consists of a short, dense, and silky under-fur as well as longer, coarser, and glossy guard hairs.

They paddle in the water with their partly-webbed hind feet and steer with their scaly tail. Muskrats are excellent swimmers. Female muskrats are the same size or slightly smaller than male muskrats. Muskrats; have a plump, rat-shaped body and has small ears and eyes that are hidden within the fur. The muskrat has small fore feet on short legs which are used for grasping food, burrowing and lodge building. The hind feet are partially webbed and aid in swimming.

The tail is scaly, black, and flattened vertically so that it can be used as a rudder while swimming. Their skull contains sixteen teeth of which four are large incisors. Two of the incisors are located on the upper anterior jaw and two on the lower anterior jaw and are very efficient when used for cutting plant material.

The common muskrat first appeared in North America approximately 1.8 million years ago. Within this time period, it has become distributed throughout suitable habitats in most of North America and is one of the most widely distributed mammals within North America.

The muskrat is rarely found in the extreme Northeast, Florida, central Texas, Mexico, and parts of California.

The muskrats require a marshy area in which to live, which is typically, a fresh or salt water marsh, marshy area of a lake or a slow-moving body of water. The water depth should be approximately 6½ feet. At this depth water will not fully freeze in winter and is shallow enough that vegetation gets adequate sunlight to successfully grow. The muskrat prefers areas with cattails, pondweeds and bulrushes since these types of vegetation provide food and building materials for the muskrat.

If this type vegetation is not present, the muskrat requires steep mud and clay banks to be able to make a burrow or underground home. Fast moving water or water bodies that change in depth too quickly do not make suitable year-round habitat, however, muskrats may occupy them for a short period of time.

Muskrats derive their name because of the two special musk glands situated just under the skin in the region of the anus. These specialized glands enlarge during the breeding season and will produce a yellowish, musky-smelling substance that is probably a means of communication during the breeding season.

The muskrat possesses special features suited to its mainly aquatic environment, which the ability to stay underwater for up to fifteen minutes (through specially adapted eyes, nose and respiratory system), waterproof fur, rudder-like tail and front teeth that allow the muskrat to chew underwater without drowning.

DISRUPT THEIR FOOD SOURCE
Muskrats rely on several aquatic vegetation and small animals to stay well fed in an area. If your pond has lush vegetation composed of cattails, water lilies, and a variety of pond weeds then you may want to clear these up and by doing so you will disrupt their diet and hopefully cause them to seek "greener" pastures. There are safe, natural chemicals to get rid of these plants or you can try the more tedious method and take them out manually.

CHANGE THE DEPTH
Muskrats prefer ponds with water depths of at least five to six feet with water that is still or very slow-moving. While there's little you can do about changing the depth of your pond, you can add an aeration system instead with a system that pumps air from a compressor located on the shore to a diffuser plate on the pond's bottom.

The induction of air through the diffuser causes a continual current (which they hate) to circulate through the entire pond. The system also controls the formation of weeds that muskrats feed on giving you a double whammy!

FENCING IS EFFECTIVE

Fencing is probably one of the most effective ways of preventing muskrats from ever taking up residence in your pond. Make sure that the fence is at least two feet high and six inches deep so they can't burrow under it. The only downside to fencing is that it can somewhat expensive, especially if your pond area is big.

TRAP 'EM!

You can also try trapping muskrats if you have some experience in doing so! You can purchase animal traps in hunting or farm supply stores. Bait the traps with apples and peanut butter. If you catch a muskrat and you want to relocate it at least one mile from your area.

COLLAPSING TUNNELS

If you can uncover muskrat tunnels you may be able to run them off by collapsing the tunnels. This will not make them happy and have an effect on their lifestyle, eating patterns and traveling patterns. It might also keep your pond from being drained, which is possible.

OPOSSOMS

JUST HANGING AROUND

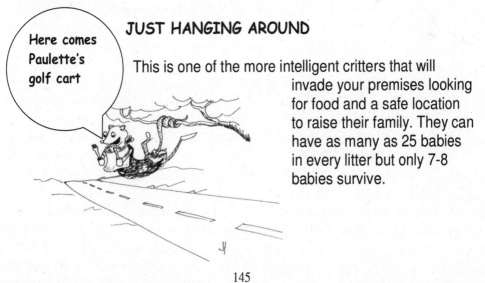

Here comes Paulette's golf cart

This is one of the more intelligent critters that will invade your premises looking for food and a safe location to raise their family. They can have as many as 25 babies in every litter but only 7-8 babies survive.

The possum is not a good climber and tends to fall out of trees. Their favorite food is roadkill and they will wait by the side of the road until you hit an animal so that they can have dinner.

They are not fussy eaters and will also indulge in your compost pile and all types of vegetables.

They love fruit when it is handy and will invade a trashcan if you leave it where they can get to it. When trapping possums be sure and wear heavy gloves since they are known to carry rabies.

OPOSSOM FACTS
- Fossil records have proven that they lived 70 million years ago during the Mesozoic Era in the late Cretaceous period.
- Adults weigh about 5 to 15 pounds, while newborns are about the size of a honey bee.
- Their life span is 3 years in the wild and about 5-7 years in captivity.
- They are often mistaken for a large rat; however, they are not members of the rodent family since they are marsupials.
- They have 52 teeth, which is more than any other mammal in North America
- Opossums are the only marsupial that is native to North America.
- Opossum fur can be white or black, but they are usually gray.
- Older opossums usually have a brown or red tone to their fur.
- Opossums are solitary, nocturnal and can live wherever there is food, water and shelter.
- They can strike surprisingly fast like and bite you before you know what happened.
- They are able to swim.
- Opossums are excellent climbers and use their hands, feet and tail to grasp.
- Their prehensile tail is used for climbing and carrying nesting materials. Both males and females build nests.
- Young opossums are able to hang upside down by their tails, but only for a short period of time.
- Their sense of smell and hearing are excellent but their eyesight is poor.
- As omnivores, they will eat anything; frogs, snails, mice, snakes, most bugs, fruit, even road killed animals.

- They mate once a year and have two litters: usually one in spring and one in late summer.
- Gestation period is only 13 days.
- Their litter can consist of as many as 25 babies then they all make their way into the pouch.
- The first 13 babies that are able to attach to a nipple survive, they rest usually die.
- Opossums are immune to rattle snake venom, rabies and distemper.
- They do not gnaw or chew on anything, dig up gardens or attack people and pets.
- They are very hardy creatures and often recover fully from illness and injury. However, since they are slow moving, they often cannot escape predators.
- To scare off attackers, they show off their sharp teeth, growl and drool - as a last resort, they will play dead "Play Possum."
- While "playing possum," they emit a foul smelling substance from their anal gland, which smells like rotten meat. This makes the opossum look like a rotting carcass and most predators will not eat them.

ALERT! POSSUM IN THE HOUSE

If an opossum gets into your house and you know where it is, you need to trap the opossum. They are harmless animals and all you need to do is chase the animal out of your house.

If necessary almost any food can be used as bait if you need to trap them. Since they are omnivores they will eat almost anything. However, be careful, although possums are usually not aggressive, they may attack and bite if they feel threatened.

EASILY TRAPPED

Possums are easily trapped, even though they are considered smart. When they see food as bait they tend to enter almost any trap to get at the food. Relocation is possible if you call the local animal control officer.

RABBITS

General Information

Rabbits and hares can have as many as 4-6 litter's, per year. Rabbits in the wild only live for 1-3 years and usually only 3-4 years in captivity.

They love vegetables and prefer carrots, peas, lettuce, beans, beets and flowers but will a variety of foods. If they have trouble finding wild food they will visit your garden regularly. There are a few crops that rabbits don't like and will stay away from. These include squash, tomatoes, corn, cucumbers, peppers and potatoes. If these are bothered it will not be from rabbits.

RABBIT FACTS

- ➢ Rabbits are not members of the rodent family.
- ➢ A male rabbit is called a buck and the female rabbit is a doe, a baby rabbit is a kit.
- ➢ When the doe gives birth her babies are collectively referred to as a litter.
- ➢ The gestation period for a rabbit averages 31 days.
- ➢ A rabbit's teeth never stop growing.
- ➢ There are 45 recognized breeds of rabbits.
- ➢ Rabbits can be litter trained just like cats.
- ➢ Domesticated rabbits need exercise to stay healthy and time outside a cage to run.
- ➢ Rabbits in captivity as pets can live as long as 10-15 years.
- ➢ Rabbits can purr similar to a cat.
- ➢ Rabbit meat is lower in fat, cholesterol and calories than chicken, pork or beef.
- ➢ Domesticated rabbits are very social and do best as when adopted in pairs. They can also bond with cats, dogs and guinea pigs with proper supervision and patience.
- ➢ Rabbit meat is all white meat.
- ➢ When bunnies become adult rabbits they can exhibit aggressive and territorial behavior. They will spray urine, mark territory with their feces, bite and grunt.
- ➢ Rabbit droppings make an excellent fertilizer.
- ➢ Rabbits have 28 teeth.

- A 4 pound rabbit will drink as much water as a 20 pound dog.
- Rabbits can jump 3 feet and higher.
- When rabbits are happy, they tend to jump and twist, this is called a "binky."
- Rabbits can learn their names and simple words such as "No."
- Predators can literally scare a rabbit to death.
- Rabbits require a solid floor in their cage instead of a wire grate since their feet are not padded like a dog or cat.
- Rabbits are not Hares, but they are closely related. Hares have fur when they are born and their eyes are open whereas rabbits are born blind and furless. "Jackrabbits" are hares.

POOR BUGS, NO CARROTS TODAY
A galvanized chicken wire fence works great providing it is sturdy and is placed about 1 foot underground and 3 feet above ground. It is best to angle the bottom 6 inches outward to stop the rabbit from digging under the fence. Chicken wire also works around the bottom of trees since rabbits like to munch on the bark.

PUT UP A BARRIER
A very effective method of keeping rabbits away from your vegetable garden is to build a cylindrical barrier enclosure. It should be about 3 feet high around all trees and plants and use ¼ inch hardware cloth then bury the bottom of the enclosure 3 inches below the ground. Make sure there is 1-2 feet between the barrier and the plants. You can also build a 3-foot high fence of chicken wire since rabbits are not good climbers.

GET SPICY WITH THEM
A mixture of ground black pepper with a dash of cayenne pepper and some bone meal sprinkled around the areas should repel the rabbits. This may upset any pets you have as well but it does work on rabbits. Best to apply just after the sun goes down since rabbits prefer evening dining.

THE RABBIT TRAPPER
Trapping rabbits is easy; the problem is what to do with them once you trap them. It is against the law to release them where they will become someone else's pest so you have to come up with a good idea.

They also tend to injure themselves trying to escape, which means now you have an injured animal to contend with. If you live in the country you may try and make rabbit stew, however, wild rabbit is a little tough to chew.

PLANT A DETERRENT
If you plant a border of wormwood around the area you want to keep rabbits out of it should work great. Rabbits hate wormwood and will avoid it at all costs. Another deterrent is to just plant a row of lettuce where they can easily get to it. Many farmers find that this works great. They may even allow you to take some occasionally.

WOOD ASHES WORK GREAT
If you sprinkle wood ashes around your plants the rabbits will leave them alone. The only problem is that when it rains the wood ashes will lose their effectiveness and you will need to add more.

TALK RADIO
If you purchase an inexpensive small portable radio and place it in the garden covered with a protective plastic bag it will keep almost all the critters away. Animals that invade the garden are afraid that there is a human around.

GET A SNAKE
Rabbits are deathly afraid of snakes and will stay away, far away from your property if they see anything that resembles a snake. Rubber fake snakes are easy to purchase and tend to be an effective deterrent.

RABBITS LOVE SAPLINGS
Rabbits love to nibble on tender saplings and one of the best ways to stop them is to wrap the sapling with a piece of plastic pipe. Be sure and leave enough room for growth. There are also a number of commercial products that can be used to wrap the saplings. Most garden supply stores carry the wraps.

A LITTLE SHMEAR WILL DO YA
A very effective method of keeping rabbits and mice away from young trees and their tender bark is to smear some bacon grease or any other animal fat on the trunk of the tree to deter them.

SAVE THOSE CONTAINERS
When rabbit presence is only occasional, new plants can be protected by using 1-gallon plastic milk containers that have the bottom cut out and placed over the seedling.

SPACE AGE TECHNOLOGY
If you hang aluminum strips on string tied to wooden stakes that are 3 feet high it will scare the critters away.

RACCOONS

General Information:
These night raiders attack during the night and love garbage cans and pet food, when left outside. They can pry open almost any garbage can and are capable of springing traps and taking the bait without being caught in them. They are not fussy about what they will eat and consume insects, snails, vegetables, eggs, mice and even crayfish. Their favorite food is sweet corn with melons coming in a close second. They can even be found under chicken coops looking for grubs. They will eat chickens by biting off their heads and pulling the body's apart.

Raccoons occasionally venture out during daytime if they are hungry or if something happened to their den. The coloring of raccoons can vary quite a bit, but the mask shaped area around the eyes is always a little darker than the rest of the coloring, giving the raccoon the look of a "bandit".

There has never been a case of rabies recorded being transmitted from a raccoon to a human.

The raccoon is a native of North and South America having a range that extends from Southern Canada to Argentina.

Raccoons have relatives also living in Europe, especially Germany, where they escaped from fur coat farms. When the farms no longer raised them for their fur, they were set loose and hunted for sport during the time around World War II.

There are 6 species of raccoon, but there are not many traits that differentiate them. Their average weight ranges from 14-16 pounds, with raccoons in colder territories, having a heavier coat weighing considerably more. Adult raccoons don't have few predators, except man, who hunts them for fur and meat.

They prefer wooded territory, which must be close to water, however, raccoons have no problem surviving in urban areas and as human populations have spread they can survive in less hospitable areas. Raccoons usually nest in tree hollows or empty underground dens left by other critters but will also make their home in abandoned cars, sewers or your chimney and are very adaptive.

Raccoons are very intelligent and have a manual dexterity that comes close to that of primates. With their long delicate fingers they can easily open clam shells, trash cans and your door. Raccoons never hibernate, but will feed heavily in the fall, storing extra fat so they can remain in their burrows through the worst parts of winter.

COON FACTS
> The heaviest raccoon recorded weighed in at a whopping 62 pounds.
> Raccoons have a very keen sense of touch.
> Raccoons never occupy a den more than 1,200 feet from a permanent water source.
> The word "raccoon" is derived from the Algonquin Indians and means "he scratches with his hands".
> Raccoons can easily open and unlock doors.
> If you give a raccoon a sugar cube, it will first try to clean it since they always wash their food and will end up washing it and washing it until the sugar cube finally dissolves to nothing.
> The record life span for a captive raccoon is 21 years, shorter in the wild.
> Raccoons are very clean animals and use a common latrine in the wild.
> Raccoons have opposable thumbs and have 40 teeth.

- They never build their own dens, they use abandoned ones.
- Raccoons are diurnal, meaning that they live above ground or below ground or even in trees.

A LITTLE BIT WILL GO A LONG WAY
Raccoons tend to look for an easy meal before they have to work for one. If you sprinkle some hydrated lime around the garbage cans it will keep them away. A little ammonia or any hot sauce placed on the lids works great too.

PHEEEW, WHAT WILL THE NEIGHBORS THINK
If you hang some old smelly clothes on your fence or a post that is staked near their entry point it will repel them. Raccoons do not like the human smell and will avoid it at all costs.

CORN IS THEIR FAVORITE FOOD
If you are growing corn the raccoons will find it. One of the best methods of keeping them away from your corn is to sprinkle the corn with water and then dust the corn with cayenne pepper. You can also spray the corn with a solution of ½ cup of cayenne, 1 pint of water and 1 tablespoon of Ivory Liquid Soap™. Allow the mixture to stand overnight before straining and spraying.

ONLY IF YOU HAVE THE TENDER TOUCH
If you rub your hand over each ear of corn it will keep the animals away. They do not like the smell of humans. If you have a big field of corn this may not be practical unless you have plenty of time and nothing else to do.

PEEK-A-BOO
Raccoons like to look up from their meal occasionally especially if they hear a strange sound. They stand up on their hind legs for a quick peek. They prefer not to dine in areas where they cannot do this easily. Some farmers will plant pumpkin seeds among the corn, which results in large leaves. This stops the raccoons from seeing if one of their predators is coming and they will stay out of the cornfield.

SAVE YOUR POOCH'S HAIR
Raccoons do not like to be around dogs. If you have a dog groomer near you, try and get the clippings from them.

If you even offer to pay them a few dollars for hair they throw away they will probably be delighted. Spread the hair around the areas where you have problems and you will never see another raccoon or rabbit.

TRAPS WILL DO THE JOB
Traps to capture the raccoons can be purchased through many mail order houses or borrowed from your local animal control agency.

There are two popular traps the Havahart Trap™ and the Safe-N-Sound™ trap. Since raccoons have a sweet tooth the best bait is honey-soaked bread, marshmallows and peanut butter is another favorite.

NOISES WORK GREAT
Any item that makes noise will scare raccoons off. This can be a noisy windmill or pinwheel device or a portable radio. Many farmers place a portable radio in their fields with the volume turned all the way up. Hopefully your home and your neighbor's home are not too close to the field. The only cost is for batteries.

WIRE MESH YOUR PLANTS
If you have a serious problem: just place wire mesh around your plants. They don't like walking on the mesh and will not come near the plants.

SKUNKS

General Information:

Skunks really are not much trouble to most gardeners since they feed mainly on insects and small animal pests, which account for about 50% of their diet. They will, however, eat the lower ears of corn. Skunks love grubs and will dig for them in your lawn or garden making them a pest. They will eat pet food if you leave it out, which is not a bad idea since they will leave your garden alone

There are four different kinds of skunks that are found in the United States. The spotted and striped skunks are the most popular and therefore more likely to come into contact with people. The hooded and hog-nosed skunks are more, rare and can be found mostly in Arizona, New Mexico and

Texas. The spotted skunk, prefer to live in the country and spends most of its life near farms. The striped skunk is more adaptable and lives in a variety of habitats and areas.

Skunks are really easy going, retiring and non-aggressive. They try very hard to stay away from humans and have a home range of a few hundred acres at most. They are usually going about their business at night and usually by themselves, except when they are raising their babies.

They are active all year; however, in northern areas they spend the coldest parts of the winter in their dens.

Skunks consume mostly insects, many of which are pests to humans so they are therefore beneficial to have around. They will also eat plant material and prefer wild fruits, apples and corn. During the winter and spring they may eat mice and the eggs of ground-nesting birds.

Skunks are able to dig their own burrows but will also use abandoned dens or burrows of other animals, hollow logs, wood or rock piles, under buildings, hay or brush piles and trees or stumps.

The skunk's main defense, as many of us are familiar with, is a complex chemical substance that includes sulfuric acid that can be fired from either one of two independently targetable anal glands. Because of this ability, skunks will usually stand and face a threat instead of running away. This works very well with people and animals but not as well against cars. Skunks can carry rabies, but not every skunk is rabid.

CHECKING FOR OCCUPANCY
If you find a suspect den, you need to check to see if the occupancy is current. This can be done by loosely filling the hole (or holes) with soil, leaves or material such as straw. If an animal such as a skunk is present, it will easily push its way out at night and reopen the hole. If the material remains undisturbed for two or three nights (and it is not winter), it is safe to assume that the hole has been abandoned and can be permanently closed.

SKUNK FACTS

> Skunks are rabies carriers but not all skunks carry rabies. All mammals can contract rabies if infected from the bite of a rabid animal. The majority of wild animals will stay clear of skunks to avoid being sprayed, so the chance of them acquiring rabies is very rare from a bite by another species is rare.

> Skunks if not startled or defending their young will rarely spray and then give plenty of warning signals before spraying. Their spray is saved for only life-threatening situations.

> A skunk could actually go through life never spraying anything.

> Skunks cannot chase and catch fast animals such as a mouse, rat or even a chicken unless it is dead, injured or in a trap. They usually eat bird eggs, chicken eggs, babies in nests or slow chicks.

> Skunks are important to the balance of nature and will kill all types of small rodents, black widow spiders, rattlesnakes, scorpions and garden pests such as snails, crickets, gophers, grubs, cockroaches and other insects.

A PROBLEM SKUNK

Trapping a skunk should probably be left to professionals or animal control since some do carry rabies. They can be trapped; by placing the trap inside a large plastic bag, keeping it open and baiting the trap with dry cat food. Skunks are usually found in pairs and if you trap one the other will surely be around to see where their partner is.

OUTSMELLING A SKUNK

If you take some old clothes that have been worn and not washed and pour some household ammonia on them then leave them out where you expect the skunk to enter or around your garden it will repel them and they will never come back.

Skunks will remember the smell of ammonia and rarely come back to a location where they smelled the odor.

THE GARDENER'S FRIEND

They may be smelly when threatened, but these animals are one of the gardener's best friends. Hopefully they will not become a resident under your home or in a shed. They are great rodent hunters and can live on a variety of insects such as grasshoppers, cutworms, tobacco worms, potato beetles, grubs and armyworms.

SNAKES

General Information:

 There are only four poisonous snakes in the United States. These are the rattlesnake, copperhead, coral snake and the water moccasin. Snakes are one of the best controllers of rodents and should be tolerated unless you have the poisonous type on your property. Bull snakes, king snakes, boas, rat snakes and gopher snakes help keep the gopher and mole population down, which is very beneficial. Garter snakes love snails and slugs and king snakes will kill the poisonous snakes as well as rodents.

Garter, brown and green snakes will eat snails, slugs and small varmints, however, they do like a tasty earthworm occasionally, which is not good for the garden.

SNAKE FACTS

> - Snakes have no eyelids, but instead of eyelids they have a transparent scale that protects their eyes.
> - Snakes are completely deaf to any airborne sounds; however, they can pick up vibrations in their jawbones and on their scent.
> - Snakes move by using special muscles attached to their ribs.
> - If a snake is placed on a piece of glass or other smooth surface, they can still move.
> - Snakes scales on their underside can act as anchors.
> - Most snakes have 200 teeth. The teeth are used to hold their prey while they are eating them.
> - Snakes cannot chew with their teeth since they are backwards.
> - Snakes can have over 300 pairs of ribs.
> - Most snakes are excellent climbers and almost all can swim.

- The tongue of a snake is to smell with and not to taste like mammals do.
- Snakes do not have ears they are just hard to see.
- King cobra eats only snakes and rat snake is its favorite.
- King cobra is the only snake who builds a nest to lay eggs.
- Snakes can live without eating for 2-3 months.
- By looking at a snake, no one can distinguish between a male or female.
- Snakes never blink their eyes.
- Snakes do not have their own burrows, they usually rat borrows, termite mounds, hollow tree trunks or under your porch to lay eggs.
- New Zealand has no snakes at all!
- The number of deaths from snake-bites in India is estimated to be between 25,000 and 40,000 per year and is amongst the highest in the world.
- Snakes cannot learn since they lack the enlarged cerebral hemispheres found in birds and mammals, this part of the brain controls learning and thought.
- Sea snakes have no gills and must rise to the surface for air, however, they can remain underwater for several hours and can obtain dissolved oxygen from water that they swallow and eject.
- Their skin is shed periodically and usually in one piece, the frequency of shedding varies with the different species, according to the size and age of the individual.
- The big pythons can eat animals like deer and even a leopard that weighs up to about 150 pounds, but swallowing such a meal is a difficult process.
- You can't tell the age of a rattlesnake by counting its rattles since it gets a new rattle every time it sheds its skin, which can occur 1 to 6 times per year.
- The fastest moving land snake is the Black Mamba.
- The venom of the Australian Brown Snake is so powerful only 1/14,000th of an ounce is enough to kill a human.

ORGANIC DETERRANT

Snake-A-Way is the world's only EPA approved, university tested, patented snake repellent. It has been proven effective against both poisonous and non-poisonous snakes. When used and applied as directed it is safe to humans, animals and plant life. It has been universally approved and endorsed by naturalists, conservationists and ecologists.

Its efficacy reached over 83% in laboratory testing and is at almost 100% with field studies that all 4 branches of the military ran during the gulf war. Snake-A-Way utilizes the knowledge about the snake's Jacobson's organ and interference with the snake's sensory reception ability causing the snake's nervous system to temporarily shut down.

REPELLANTS DON'T REPEL
There are no snake repellants that have been tried that will work to keep snakes away from your property. A number have been tried commercially and they end up killing the snakes.

SNAKE-PROOF FENCE
It is best to use a very heavy galvanized screen about 36 inches wide and use ¼ inch mesh. You will need to bury the lower edges 2-3 inches in the ground and then slant it outward from the bottom to the top at a 30-degree angle. Your supporting stakes should be inside the fence and the gates must be tightly fitted. This is an expensive method if you have a large yard. Best to just fence in your children's play area.

WEASELS

General Information

Weasels are small, powerful carnivorous mammals with short legs and an elongated, slender body and neck in the family, Mustelidae. They are closely related to otter, badgers and polecats.

The name weasel derives from the Anglo-Saxon word "weatsop" meaning "a vicious bloodthirsty animal." There are 17 species of weasel and most live on river banks and near streams. Weasels eat frogs, rats, mice, birds, rabbits and squirrels.

Weasels can be divided into two major categories - short tailed weasels and long tailed weasels. The basic structure of their bodies; is same but are highly powerful, compared to their small size. Weasels are considered to be fearless, ferocious hunters and are not afraid to confront bigger animals.

Weasels are known to be found in areas with abundant water and will mark their territories with a pungent secretion from their anal scent glands. They are only able to live for about 2-3 years in the wild but can survive for 10 years in captivity.

The ermine and some other species are brown in summer, and turn white in winter while others are brown at all seasons. Weasels can change their coat color as a defense mechanism. Their predators are badgers, foxes and birds of prey such as the large owl and eagle.

Weasels are poisonous and the antidote for treating weasel bites is secreted only by monkeys. The collective name for a group is a boogle, gang, pack and confusion. Males are called dog, buck, Jack and hob. Females are called bitch, doe or Jill and the name given to babies are kits

WEASEL FACTS

 - ➤ Weasels are generally confused with ferrets and at times, even monkeys.
 - ➤ The weasel is native to North America, Europe and Britain.
 - ➤ These are also places where monkeys are not native.
 - ➤ "Pop goes the weasel" is a popular nursery rhyme in which weasels are mentioned. However, in reality weasels make a squelching like sound.
 - ➤ Weasels are homosexual creatures and the only reason they mate with the opposite sex is to ensure their species remains.
 - ➤ In the event a person is bitten by a weasel, he could die due to the poison if not given antidote, which is a monkey secretion.
 - ➤ Weasels are generally very lazy and this explains why they do not flee in spite of being capable.
 - ➤ One of the principal characters in the 'Ice Age' movie series, Sid, is a weasel.
 - ➤ Weasels move swiftly and are master predators. They make no sound, and approach their prey quietly, pouncing on it after getting in range.
 - ➤ Minks and ferrets are considered to be the closest relatives of weasels.
 - ➤ Weasels do not hibernate and are therefore active during summer as well as winter seasons. They are also known to be nocturnal.

- For hundreds of years the fur from a weasel has been used for making winter jackets and parkas. It is believed, in western societies, a weasel's fur was considered to be a sign of royalty.
- There have been numerous laws and restrictions laid upon the hunting and killing of weasels all over the world for fur, to protect this species from extinction.

Long Tailed Weasel Facts

- Male long tailed weasels are about 13 to 16 inches in length, bigger than the females, which are 11 to 14 inches in length.
- As the name goes, these weasels have very long tails almost half the size of their body and head put together.
- Long tailed weasels are generally found at places, which have a sizable rodent population and lots of water.
- Squirrels, voles, moles, rats, chipmunks and mice are consumed by the long tailed weasel and at times they also eat birds, insects and frogs.
- An interesting is that whenever they are ready to attack or frightened, they give away long chirps. The other type of sound is a low trilling sound, heard when two weasels of opposite sex meet.

Short Tailed Weasel Facts

- Short tailed weasels are known as stoat or ermine and are small mammals with a furry body.
- Short tailed weasels can be found in the Arctic tundra region of Europe and North America.
- These weasels have a paler color on their belly as compared to the rest of their body and the tip of their tail is mostly black. It remains black even when their fur turns white in winter.
- These weasels will also grow about 10 inches long and have tails which are around 3 inches in length. Females are smaller in size than males.
- Short tailed weasels are excellent hunters and prey on other smaller mammals like rats, rabbits and squirrels.
- A strange weasel fact is that it does not have many friends. This is because they are not too trustworthy and are often known to kill other animals without reason.
- Also, weasels are very curious mammals and are often found looking under bushes and peeping into holes in search of a prey.

BEST TO TRAP THEM

The best method of getting rid of weasels is to set humane traps. Ready-make kits are available for purchase from larger farm-supply stores or build your own using a standard spring-loaded trap and bait. Make sure the trap is in a secluded area and has a cover to reduce the risk that the weasel can step out of the trap. Once caught, safely transport the weasel to a safe place and release it into the wild. Be careful to avoid bites and scratches from the animal since a bite may be poisonous.

If you are going to trap a weasel, be sure and use a bait of fresh meat with lots of blood on it. They tend to smell the meat and come running towards it making it easier to trap them.

CLOSE OFF ALL ENTRANCES

Weasels are attracted to food. If the food is not accessible, weasels simply move on! Make sure to seal all entrances to barns or garages, there must not be any holes larger than an inch in diameter open to the outside. Erect tough barriers to outdoor chicken coops and rabbit cages so weasels (or foxes or other carnivorous predators) cannot directly attack livestock. These enclosures should have a roof.

Remove Potential Hiding Spots for Weasels

Remove all potential hiding places especially around poultry cages, chicken runs and the chicken coop. Mow any long grasses and weeds, while severely trimming shrubs and ivy. The idea is to remove anything that a weasel may be able to hide under or behind and stalk unwitting poultry. Remove any woodpiles, junk or debris that might be a hiding place for a watchful weasel.

Poultry predators are not happy to have to stalk out in the open; clearing a wide path around the poultry areas could be the entire deterrent necessary to protect the flock. Remove any greenery that prevents a straight view from a home or main building to the poultry pens and coops. This gives a farmer the ability to see a weasel and perhaps reach the coop before any savagery erupts.

Dig a trench under the chicken wire fences protecting the poultry. It should be at least 2 feet deep, as cunning weasels can dig that far to get the prize.

Submerge at least 2 feet of plywood along the edge of the fences into the trenches. For home farmers on a budget, using bricks or heavy chicken wire will work as well, as long as it reaches the required 2-foot depth, preventing unwanted visitors from burrowing under them.

Attach the boards or the wire to the fences. With wire fencing, attach with wire ties; with plywood, attach to the fence with a large staple gun. The protection to the poultry is in how secure the fence attaches to the barriers. Use wire cutters to remove any sharp points that could injure the poultry or the weasel. Humane is the name of the game.

Barbed Wire May Be A Bit Much - But It Works!
Unroll a length of razor wire or barbed wire to put on top of the poultry housing areas. This may seem like a bit of overkill, but weasels raccoons and other persistent, stubborn and intelligent predators will stop at nothing to get to the poultry. Staple the starting point of barbed or razor wire firmly to the top of each fence and the top of each poultry building, with a heavy-duty staple gun, coiling it to give it extra girth and spines that are closer together.

Secure all barbed wire or razor wire now with the heavy-duty staples, going back to the beginning where the wire was started and adding staples to ensure stability.
Follow the length and shapes of the fences and coops and trail barbed wire along them, securing them intermittently with a heavy-duty staple. Use wire cutters to remove any sharp wire that could potentially harm the poultry or the weasel.

WILD BOAR

General Information
Wild or feral boars, are wild swine from domestic ancestry, belonging to the family Suidae. There are actually three types of wild hogs found in the United States: Eurasian wild boar (Russian) and hybrids. The hybrid is a cross between the wild pig and the Russian wild boar.

California, Florida and Texas have the highest numbers of wild boar. One of the Hawaiian Islands has significant populations as well and Oklahoma's population is quickly growing.

Even though these states and many others have populations of wild pigs, they are not native to the United States. A hog-like animal, the javelina or collared peccary, is native to the southwest U.S. However, the wild boar is a different species, genus and family from the javelina which belongs to the family Tayassuidae and native to the Southwest U.S.

The javelina is often confused with the wild boar. Javelinas are hog-like in appearance; however, they are not closely related. Relatives of our swine date back to the Miocene. During the period when the world was shifting and forming new continents, the swine family was excluded from the new world. It was probably not until the discovery of the new world by European man that swine found their way into what is now the U.S.

Early explorers such as Hernando Cortes and Hernando De Soto are for the most part largely responsible for their introduction. The swine these explorers brought over were domesticated and it was not until the 1930's that the Russian wild boar was introduced.

Today, there are areas in the U.S. where the pure Russian wild boar can still be found due to its importation for sport hunting. However, most wild boar, are from domesticated swine. Feral hogs are in fact wild pigs but are not a different species than domestic hogs or Russian boars. Webster's dictionary defines feral as: having escaped from domestication and become wild. Hence, all feral hogs in the U.S. up until the 1930's were from domestic stock. In a few areas where the Russian boar was imported for sport hunting, escapes have occurred resulting in feral Russian crossbreeding.

WILD BOAR FACTS
 - ➢ A wild boar can reach three feet in height and over 800 pounds in weight.
 - ➢ The average sow weighs approximately 110 pounds and the average boar weighs 130 pounds.
 - ➢ A boar has four continually growing tusks that can be extremely sharp and may reach five inches in length before they are broken or worn down from use.
 - ➢ Tusks are used for defense and to establish dominance during breeding.

- A male wild boar also develops a thick, tough skin composed of cartilage and scar tissue on the shoulder area which is sometimes referred to as a shield.
- The boar's shield develops continually as the hog ages and through fighting.
- Tusks which are found on the lower jaw, or mandible, can be extremely dangerous when put to use by a mature boar.
- The upper tusks, or whittlers, help keep the lower tusk extremely sharp.
- The pure Russian boar is generally light brown or black with a cream or tan color on the tips of its bristles. Its underside is lighter in color and its legs, ears and tail are darker than the rest of the coat. Its bristles are the longest of the three types of wild hogs.
- Pure Russian boars have longer legs and snouts and their head to body ratio is much greater than a feral hog. They also tend to have shorter, straighter tails.
- States with wild boar: 39, not including 4 Canadian provinces.
- Texas Counties with Feral Hogs: 225 out of 254 counties.
- Hog Population in Texas: 2,000,000.
- National Population: estimated around 4,000,000.
- Estimated Annual Agricultural Damage in Texas from feral swine: $52 million.
- Landowner Annual Expense to control feral hogs in Texas: $7 million.
- Natural Life Expectancy of a Feral Hog: 6 to 8 years.
- Their main way of communicating is by using sounds, smells and visual signals like the position of the tail and ears.
- These animals are active both during day and night but they mostly feed during the night.
- When they are alarmed, they usually start to squeal.
  Depending on ancestry, the physical characteristics of wild boar can vary greatly. Size, shape and color can all fluctuate. And all types of wild swine can raise their hair on the back of their necks giving them the look of a razorback.
- Feral/Russian crosses exhibit combinations of features from both the feral and the Russian hogs. Bristle length in the hybrid is longer than the feral but shorter than the Russian.

- Hybrids exhibit the smallest bristle shaft diameters. Striped patterns on the young are sometimes thought to be an indicator of pure Russian or feral/Russian crosses; however, this pattern has also been found in feral piglets and therefore is not a reliable method of identification.
- A feral hogs' sense of smell is very, underrated. It is known that wild boars have a highly developed, acute sense of smell.
- A wild boars' sense of smell rivals that of even deer and when placing traps or such, our human scent is left lingering. The human scent can last for days on an item. After your scent wears off the trap then and usually only then, will the wild hogs come into the trap!
- Even if the trap is baited, the boars will not touch the trap nor the food in it if it carries the strong human scent that was left behind when being placed.
- These animals aren't easily captured because their intelligence makes it that more difficult to capture them.
- To capture wild boars, you must be prepared to put in the effort. You have to have the patience to wait days on end for one to take the bait. You must be prepared to continually move your traps because the hogs will remember where you've caught other hogs, and stay away. I wish capturing wild hogs was as simple as setting out a baited trap and hauling them in, but alas, they just aren't that easy!

FENCING WORKS, BUT IS EXPENSIVE, BEST TO TRAP!

The best method for keeping feral hogs out of any area is fencing, which is expensive. The next-best method is to get the hogs feeding regularly inside a trap to accustom them to going into the trap night after night for several weeks. Then, set the trap with a hard trigger to hopefully catch every hog possible in the herd when the door on the trap falls.

PIG SPRAY!

If you find large chunks of turf torn up from your lawn, it is most likely a wild boar, especially if you live in a rural area. One of the best methods to get rid of the wild boars and other small animal is to use motion detecting sprinklers or lighting. This, an inexpensive way to go and will not hurt the animals.

MESH TO THE RESCUE!

Surround your garden with fine plastic mesh. Just lay it low on the ground so that it is 2 to 4 inches above the soil. Plants will still grow through the mesh, but it will work as a barrier. Wild boar will not bother an area where their feet may become entangled.

BEGONE, GRUBS!

Wild boar love to dig for grubs and will not frequent an area that does not have any. To eliminate grubs from your lawn just purchase some beneficial nematodes and apply them to your lawn. The soapy water sprayed on your lawn may also kill off the grubs as well as a strong garlic spray and will not harm the soil. Apply it when the sun is high in the sky and earthworms are deep in the soil since you do not want to kill off the earthworms..

WILD TURKEY

General Information

Wild turkeys are birds of that live in the woods. These birds require an area from a few hundred acres to more than a thousand acres of ground with a numerous of trees for roosting, a reliable water source and an open feeding area so they can remain aware of predators. In spring and summer, when the birds are nesting and raising broods,

Birds in the East generally inhabit very dense forests and river bottomlands usually adjacent to agricultural lands. Birds in the West and South prefer pine and oak forests near streams. Florida birds are usually found in oak and pine woods, palmetto flats and cypress bottomlands.

Wild turkeys will move seasonally between nesting and wintering areas, but rarely travel more than two miles. In mountainous areas, wild turkeys live at higher elevations in spring and summer, and lower elevations in fall and winter and sometimes move as much as forty miles between ranges.

Wild turkeys consume mostly plant material, including fruits, acorns and other nuts, small grains, seeds, shoots and roots of grasses and various other plants. They also eat numerous types of insects, small amphibians and even a lizard or two.

Turkeys generally fly down from roosting trees to feed in early morning, and return to the safety of the trees in the evening.

Wild turkey toms start their breeding displays in early spring while they are still gathered in flocks in the wintering areas. Their tail fanned, feathers fluffed and with their wing tips dragging, the tom struts around boldly while emitting low-pitched sounds. He repeats this display, coupled with his characteristic gobble call, until he attracts a suitable hen.

The most dominant toms will breed with the most hens, continuing to display after each mated hen goes off to nest. By late spring, breeding is nearly complete and the males lose their desire. The hen becomes very secretive at nesting time and will distance herself from other hens.

The nesting site is usually under or near a log, bush or clump of vegetation. She will scrape a shallow depression, line it with leaves and twigs then lays 8 to 14 speckled eggs, which hatch in about 27 days.

Wild turkeys are capable of running over 20 miles per hour and fly up to speeds of 40 miles per hour.

There are five subspecies of wild turkey in North America they are:

> ➤ The Eastern wild turkey, which is the most abundant of the five subspecies and is found throughout most of the eastern United States. Its population is increasing in the Pacific Northwest and North Dakota. It has a copper-bronze sheen, and its tail has a chocolate-brown tip.
> ➤ Merriam's wild turkey, which is found in areas of the western United States, from Montana to Arizona. It is the most adaptable of the five subspecies and its numbers have increased as well as its range due to stocking efforts. It has a purplish bronze sheen, and a buff-tipped tail.
> ➤ The Rio Grande wild turkey is found primarily in the south-central United States from Nebraska through Texas. Its range has moved westward thanks due stocking efforts. The overall body sheen is a pale copper, and the tail has a yellowish tip.

- The Florida wild turkey is found only in Florida, and has a small, fairly stable population. It looks similar in appearance to the eastern wild turkey, but has darker wings and a somewhat iridescent, greenish gold body color. It tends to hybridize with the eastern turkey, where the ranges of the two subspecies overlap.
- Gould's wild turkey is found in extreme southern Arizona and New Mexico. It looks similar to the Merriam's subspecies, but has a bluish green sheen and a white-tipped tail.

WILD TURKEY FACTS
- Courtship begins in late March and early April.
- Egg laying starts around mid-April and peak of nest incubation is normally the first week of May.
- Hatching takes place 28 days later, normally during the first week of June.
- Acorns are wild turkeys favorite foods.
- Wild turkeys have a poor sense of smell and taste and normally select acorns based on their size and shape.
- Wild turkey beards will grow throughout the life of the bird and usually grow about 4 inches every year.
- Juvenile males or "Jakes" usually have a beard that is about 2-4 inches in length by the end of their first year.

- Adult males or "Toms" commonly sport beards that are 8-12 inches in length.
- The overall length of the beard is regulated by wear as the beard drags the ground.
- Hens can have beards and on rare occasions they even have spurs.
- Spurs have a bony core and are covered with a keratinous material similar to our fingernails.
- Spurs grow throughout the life of the bird and can be used to estimate age.
- Due to overhunting and deforestation that eliminated wild turkeys' habitat, these birds were nearly extinct in the 1930s.
- Currently, there are more than 7 million wild turkeys.
- There are approximately 5,500 feathers on an adult wild turkey.
- The average lifespan of a wild turkey is 3-5 years, and the oldest known wild turkey lived to be at least 13.

- In the wild, turkeys range from 5-20 pounds, however, domestic turkeys are specially bred to be heavier.
- Because it is a native bird with a proud demeanor and protective instincts, the wild turkey was Benjamin Franklin's choice for the national bird instead of the eagle.
- A wild turkey's gobble can be heard up to one mile away.
- Alaska and Hawaii are the only two states without extensive wild turkey populations.
- The wild turkey's bald head can change color in seconds with excitement or emotion. The birds' heads can be red, pink, white or blue.
- Wild turkeys see in color and have excellent daytime vision that is three times better than a human's eyesight and covers 270 degrees, but they have poor vision at night.

SOLUTIONS TO WILD TURKEYS

The best solutions are to either get a dog to chase them away or to fence them out. The only other solution is to have them for Thanksgiving dinner and trap them.

WOLF

General Information

Wolves are in a class of the canine family, in fact, they are the largest of all canines. They are meat eaters and can range in size depending on where they live. Some wolves are only about 50-60 pounds full grown, while others can be up to 200 pounds. They range in size from 4½ feet to 6 feet when measured from the tip of the nose to the end of the tail.

Wolves have long gotten a bad reputation in the wild; however, they are very intelligent animals that live in groups, known as packs. They have very thick fur, which helps them survive in a variety of climates.

They are found to live in many places throughout the Northern Hemisphere, however, the amount of roaming space that they have continues to grow smaller all the time.

Wolf packs can have from 6 to 20 members in them at any one time. They have a very large range that they cover, which can extend up to 15 miles. They hunt as a group, which makes it possible for them to take down large prey such as deer, moose and elk. This type of kill helps to ensure there is plenty of food to go around for the entire pack.

Other than hunting to eat, wolves are usually not aggressive; however, they are often pictured that way. They will fight other animals and even other wolves in order to protect their pack. This is where the stories often come in of wolves being violent killers. The biggest threat is to them and not to other animals or humans. The reduction of their habitat has created a great deal of hardship for the wolves.

The average lifespan of a wolf in the wild is from 6 to 8 years. However, in captivity they can live up to 16 years and they don't seem to have a problem adjusting to life in captivity. Most of the locations where they are kept try to keep the habitat as natural as they possibly can for them.

It is illegal in many areas to sell the pelts of the wolf. However, they were once worth a great deal of money and some still circulate on the black market.

In the United States wolves were almost hunted to the point of extinction. Breeding programs with the Red Wolves have allowed them to start to repopulate. In the 1980's they were literally wiped out in the wild, with those remaining only in captivity. Through programs to introduce them to new environments they now live in North Carolina. Approximately 100 of them are found there at this point in time.

There have been efforts in Colorado and other states to reintroduce certain species of wolves to special locations. So far those programs have been successful. However, it may not be enough to help get these animals off the list of endangered species any time soon.

Wolves have a very complex social structure that has been carefully studied. There is a different hierarchy for both the males and the females that belong to it. Contrary to popular belief, there isn't constant fighting within a pack to get to the top of the rankings. Instead this type of social structure actually helps to keep the focus on survival for the entire pack.

WOLF FACTS

- The coyote evolved separately from the wolf over 500,000 years ago.
- The wolf has 42 teeth, rounded ears and a broad heavy muzzle.
- Wolves have extremely powerful jaws capable of generating 1,500 psi of pressure.
- Wolves have one of the widest ranges of size, shape and color of any mammal in North America.
- Loss of habitat and persecution by humans are leading factors in the Wolves "Endangered Species Status."
- Wolves have large feet, the average being 4 inches wide by 5 inches long.
- Wolves breed once a year, December through March, depending on latitude, the gestation period is 63 days.
- Wolf pups are born in northern climates as late as early June and in southern climates as early as late February and the average litter size are 4 to 6 cubs.
- The cubs weigh approximately one pound at birth and cannot see or hear.
- Pack Territories vary with location. In the Alaskan or Canadian Wilderness the territory for one pack ranges from 300 to 1,000 square miles while in the continental U.S. the territory is between 25 and 150 square miles.
- A Wolf in a hurry can go as fast as 35 miles per hour for short distances.
- The Wolves' diet of choice consists of deer, moose, caribou, elk, bison, musk-oxen and beaver. They have been known to survive on voles and mice if need be.
- The wolf lives in a pack, family oriented social structure.
- Wolves have a vast communication repertoire including scent marks, vocalizations, visual displays, facial and body postures and rituals.
- Wolves communicate with each other more by harmony and integration rather than by aggression and submission.
- Wolves are territorial and defend their territory through vocalizations and scent marking.
- There are two species of the wolf in North America, the Gray Wolf (*Canis lupus*) and the Red Wolf (*Canis rufus*).
- In North America there are 10 recognized sub-species of the wolf.
- The wolf is an ultimate predator at the top of the food chain.

- The wolf primarily travels at a 5 mile per hour trot, however, in chases, wolves can achieve estimated speeds of between 28 and 40 miles per hour for up to 20 minutes.
- Radio tracking wolves has been used in wildlife research since 1963.
- Wolves are vulnerable to skull injury from kicking prey.
- The canine teeth "interlock" so the wolf can grip and hang on to struggling prey.
- The back teeth, or carnassial molars, are designed to crush bones and shear meat.
- The wolf has 2 types of hair, "Guards and "Undercoat."
- The wolf's sense of smell is more than 100 times greater than a human.
- The "Alpha" wolf is the highest ranking individual within the dominance hierarchy. The "beta" wolf is the second ranking individual within the dominance hierarchy and the "omega" wolf is the lowest ranking individual within the dominance hierarchy.
- In the winter, the wolf's tail helps keep their face warm.
- In addition to howling, wolves bark, yap, whine, and growl.
- All members of a wolf pack take part in caring for the young.
- When pack members return from the hunt and they are nipped on the snout by the pups, the hunters regurgitate undigested meat for them.
- Although wolves are feared throughout much of the world, documented attacks on people are extremely rare.
- A wolf can consume almost twenty pounds of prey at a feeding.

CALL A PROFESSIONAL
The only sure method of getting rid of wolves in your area is to call a professional and go by their recommendations. Wolves normally will not bother you unless they are starving and can't find food.

WOLVERINE

General Information
Wolverines are very territorial animals and have the muscular strength and ferocity to defend it. Although weighing in at just about 29 pounds it is said that the wolverine has the ability of defending its food from wolf packs, mountain lions and even bears. They are believed to be the strongest animal for their size amongst mammals.

Although the wolverine resembles a small-sized bear, it is actually the largest species of the weasel family. Its fur is brownish-black with light brown strips along the sides. The fur is dense and long and will resist water, which helps the wolverine tolerate the cold conditions in environment it inhabits.

Wolverines usually live to between 8 and 13 years old, however, some wolverines in captivity have been known to nearly reach the age of 20! The wolverine is considered to be a near threatened species as the wolverine numbers are declining due to hunting and habitat loss.

Wolverines have a stocky build, powerful limbs, a large head, a short tail and small ears. Its feet are equipped with pads that enable it to travel easily through deep heavy snow, and it also has large claws. It is basically a solitary animal and requires a lot of space to roam and have been known to journey 15 miles a day in search of food. Some animals have been tracked over the snow for 40-60 miles.

They will track caribou herds when they migrate and feed off the carcasses, that bears and wolves have left behind, using their strong jaws to crush the bones.

Because of their need for large ranges of habitat, wolverines can be found in the remote regions of Canada, Europe, parts of North America and the Arctic Circle where the wolverines inhabit mountainous regions and dense forests. Wolverines are also known to venture into more open areas such as plains and farmland when they are in search of food.

Wolverines are basically a terrestrial animal; however, they are very good at climbing trees and are also excellent swimmers. They have great stamina and use a fast pace, traveling great distances without a break.

Wolverines are similar to other weasels in that the wolverine by nature is curious, daring and very tough. They are an omnivorous animal, feeding on a wide variety of food and in the summer will eat berries, edible roots, and various plants. However, being vicious predators, they will travel great distances to get its preferred food, meat!

Smaller sized prey, like mice, rats and rabbits, is easy fare for the wolverine, if the opportunity presents itself, it will attack animals that are much larger in size, like deer, elk and caribou, especially if they are injured or weak. Wolverines are also opportunistic feeders that eat animals which have been killed by other predatory animals. Eating carrion helps them to survive the winter, when food is usually scarce. They will even dig into the snow to find and eat hibernating animals.

They are mainly nocturnal animals, however, if the wolverine finds itself in regions of extended darkness or daylight, it tends to change to a pattern of being awake for 4 hours and sleeping for 4 hours. Similar to the bear, the wolverine has poor eyesight, however, its hearing and sense of smell are very good. Like the skunk, the wolverine has a strong-smelling fluid called musk which the wolverine uses to warn others to stay away.

The male wolverine uses their scent glands to mark their territory and will sometimes even mark their caches of food. They are polygamous and have been known to share their territory with a number of females.

Even though wolverines are solitary animals, members of the family do play with each other. Female wolverines will dig underground to give birth to their young, which usually are 2 to 3 at a time, either in early spring or late winter. Usually the young will live with their mother until they are two years of age, which is the age that they mature enough to reproduce themselves.

Scientists have a hard time studying wild wolverines because these animals are shy, hard to find, and roam over large, out-of-the-way wilderness areas. Scientists also worry about the future of wolverines since these animals need large areas of wilderness to survive and as people move into what was once wilderness, their way of life is threatened.

CALL A PROFESSIONAL
Wolverines normally will not be a pest in urban areas, however, if one does appear it would be best to call a professional for help. However, if they do appear, they will probably leave before anyone gets there. Be sure and keep all small animals indoors or fenced in till the threat is gone.

CHAPTER 20

BIRDS

BIRDS

General Information:

Because of the number of insects birds consume, they are considered very beneficial to your yard and especially the garden. There are many birds that you should try and attract to your property. However, to attract the right birds you will need to feed foods that they prefer and build them houses that they can reside in. Some of the foods recommended are for indoor bird pets as well as outdoor wild birds.

BIRD FOOD

CANARY FOOD

The following ingredients will be needed:

1	Ounces of dried egg yolk
1	Ounce of powdered poppy heads
1	Ounce of powdered cuttlefish bone
2	Ounces of granulated sugar

Place all the ingredients into a small bowl and mix well. Store the feed in a well-sealed container in a cool dry location.

PARROT GRIT

The following ingredients will be needed:

1	Teaspoon of coarse, sharp sand
1	Teaspoon of powdered charcoal (fine)
1	Teaspoon of ashes (filtered and clean)
1	Teaspoon of flowers of sulfur

Place all the ingredients into a sifter and sift together, then keep a portion of the mixture in the parrot's cage at all times.

MAKING MIXED BIRDSEED

The following ingredients will be needed:

6	Ounces of canary seed
2	Ounces of rapeseed
1	Ounces of Maw seed
2	Ounces of millet seed

Place all the seeds in a jar and shake well. This formula is mainly for wild birds.

MAKING MOCKINGBIRD FOOD
The following ingredients will be needed:

2	Ounces of cayenne pepper
8	Ounces of rapeseed
16	Ounces of hemp seed
2	Ounces of corn meal
2	Ounces of rice
8	Ounces of crushed cracker
2	Ounces of lard oil

Place the first 6 ingredients into a bowl and crush into a powder, then add the oil and blend well.

MAKING CARDINAL FOOD
The following ingredients will be needed:

8	Ounces of sunflower seed
16	Ounces of hemp seed
10	Ounces of canary seed
8	Ounces of wheat
6	Ounces of rice

Place all the ingredients into a bowl and grind into a powder.

HOW TO ATTRACT BIRDS

BARN SWALLOW
These birds like an area where there is available water and mud and you must provide straw for their nests. They like a 6"X6" shelve for their nesting support and it needs to be 8-12 feet above the ground. They like eaves and well-protected areas.

BARN SWALLOW

BLUEBIRD

These birds like a birdbath that is high enough off the ground so that cats can't get to it. They prefer mulberry, holly, blueberry, wild cherry and Virginia creeper plants to munch on. They are fussy about their birdhouses and they would prefer a 5"X5"X8" birdhouse with 1½" entry holes about 6 inches above the floor. If you place the nest 5 feet off the ground it will discourage the sparrows; who prefer nest that are higher up.

CHICKADEE

They prefer a diet of peanut butter, suet, sunflower seeds and some breadcrumbs. Their birdhouse should be 4"X4"X8" with the holes 1 1/8th inches and should be 6 inches above the floor. The house needs to be 8-15 feet high.

KESTREL

Wild birdseed is their favorite, a good mix will do. Their birdhouse should be 8"X8"X12" with a 3 inch hole that is 9-12 inches above the floor. It should be at least 10 feet above the ground but not more than 30 feet.

KINGLET

Kinglet's prefers to eat suet, wild birdseed, cracked nuts and raw peanuts. They also like to nest in conifers preferably near the northern gardens.

MOCKINGBIRD (from the hill)

These birds are fussy and insist on a nice birdbath and attractive surroundings. They prefer to eat crab apples, cherry, blueberries, grapes and blackberries. However, they won't turn down a meal of dogwood; pasture rose, red cedar, elderberry, mulberry, manzanita and Virginia creeper.

OWL (old hooty)

They prefer to nest in large shade trees, oak trees or conifers. If they find a dead tree with a hollow hole they will reside there before almost any other location. They are night hunters and eat rodents and prefer a grassy area to hunt in.

OWL (barn)

They are fussy and require that you build them a nesting box 10"X18"X16" that has a 6 inch opening and about 4 inches from the floor. They dine on rodents and small animals and like an open field or pasture nearby.

OWL (saw-whet)

You will need to build a nesting box that is 6"X6"X10" that has a 2½" entry hole that is 8 inches above the floor. The house needs to be securely fastened 15-20 feet above the ground.

OWL (screecher)

Their home must be 8"X8"X14" and have a 3 inch hole. The house must be about 12-30 feet off the ground and must be in a secluded area since they like their privacy.

PHOEBE

These birds require a nesting platform that is about 6-8 inches square and 8-12 feet off the ground. They would prefer to be under an eave or in any protected area.

PURPLE MARTIN

These are apartment dwellers but don't put the apartment house up until the Martin's arrive or the starlings will move in. You will need 15-20 small apartments measuring 6"X6"X6" with the entry hole  about 2½ inches and 1 inch from the floor. The birdhouse should be 15-20 feet off the ground. They eat wild birdseed and insects with a worm or two for dessert.

TITMOUSE

This bird will do anything for a doughnut but also loves to eat suet, nuts, sunflower seeds, peanut butter and breadcrumbs. The bird likes to be around elderberry, wild strawberry, pine, beech, mulberry and pine.

The birdhouse needs to be 4"X4"X8" and have a 1¼ inch entry hole about 6 inches off the floor. The house ideally needs to be 8-15 feet off the ground.

WARBLER

They prefer nice landscaping and pleasant surroundings (fussy bird). They will go crazy for mulberry and especially raspberries but also like wild rose, barberry, hedge, privet, grapevines, current, elder, which provide additional nesting sites.

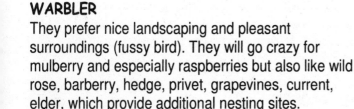

WREN

The birdhouse must be 4"X4"X6" with 1 inch holes for entry and the holes should be about 4 inches off the floor. The birdhouse should be 8-10 feet high.

Hints on Building a Birdhouse

- ❖ Don't bother with a perch since they are rarely used.
- ❖ Drill some ventilation holes just under the roofline and a few in the floor for drainage.
- ❖ The house should blend in with the scenery and not be frilly.
- ❖ The inside should be rough and even if bark is showing it is best.
- ❖ Always use screws not nails to insure the stability and quality.
- ❖ Hollowing out a small log works great as a birdhouse.
- ❖ The roof must be waterproof.
- ❖ The dimensions should be for the bird for which you are building it.
- ❖ Never use screw eyes to hang the house up since they will loosen in time.
- ❖ Hinge the bottom so that it will be easy to clean. The house needs to be cleaned after the birds leave.

- ❖ You can be creative as long as the house does not look out-of-place in its surroundings.
- ❖ If you are not handy, buy one in your garden shop.

PROBLEM BIRDS

General Information:

If birds are a problem it is best to identify which bird is really causing the problem.

Only five birds are really bad pests that will damage a garden enough to warrant going after them. They are crows, seagulls, starlings, woodpeckers and blackbirds. However, damage that looks like birds are doing it may be from raccoons or other animals.

BUZZ AROUND, BUZZ AROUND

If you want to keep all birds away from your garden and plants, try using a piece of commercial buzzing or humming tape. This tape is stretched across an area near the garden and will make noise when the wind blows to scare away the birds.

ORDER A CAT SCARECROW

Make a cutout of a cat and decorate it to look like the real thing. If birds are a problem this works great.

THE OLD HOOTY OWL

This really works better than almost any other means of keeping all birds away. Make sure that you purchase an owl with a movable head. When the wind blows the head moves around the body.

GET A SNEAKY SNAKE

Not all but most birds are afraid of snakes so you may want to purchase a realistic rubber snake or use a piece of garden hose.

PORCUPINE WIRE

There are a number of tactile repellants made to keep birds away.
They are called porcupine wires and are sold under the names of Nixalite™ and Cat Claw™. These are permanent repellants that are usually placed on windowsills, eaves, ledges and anywhere that the birds will roost.

The prongs extend outward and they can be fastened to any surface. These will cause some discomfort to the bird but will not do serious damage.

PANTYHOSE FOR SQUASH????????
If you want to keep the birds away from melons and squash, just place the squash or melon in an old pantyhose leg.

VENTS ARE PROBLEMS
Many birds tend to nest in vents, especially dryer vents. It is best to cover these vents with a netting to prevent the problem. Special plastic bird netting is available through a garden supply house or from InterNet, Inc. at (800) 328-8456.

RING-A-DING-DING
If you have a good view of your garden most of the time when at home during the day, just rig a long string to a bell and have the string where you can get to it from the house. When you see birds bothering your garden pull the string and the bell will ring and they will leave the premises.

BUILD A HOUSE FOR MARTINS
One of the best insect eaters is the purple martin. If you have them in your area and you build them a house, they will assist you in keeping your garden insect-free. It is best to obtain a book on birdhouses and build one for their special needs.

ARE BIRDS EATING YOUR CHERRIES?
Birds can be kept from eating your cherries by spraying the cherries with salt water. The birds may also be eating the cherries because they are thirsty and the cherries are an excellent source of water for them.

BIRDS PREFER TART BERRIES
If you are having a problem with birds eating your sweet berries, just plant some tart berries near the sweet ones and the bird will only eat the tart ones.

SET UP A BIRD DINER
One of the best methods of attracting birds is to place a number of feeders around your property. A good variety of different seeds will attract different birds and they will have your insects for dessert.

POPCORN FOR THE BIRDS
If you are having a problem with birds bothering your corn, they may just be after the corn earworms. However, to be on the safe side, just soak some popcorn corn overnight and throw it on the ground around you ears of corn. They prefer the easy meal instead of bothering your corn.

SAVE THOSE STRAWBERRIES
One of only ways to stop birds from consuming your strawberries is to throw some netting over the patch. Birds get scared off and think that they may get tangled up in the netting.

SAVING THE FRUIT TREES
There are a number of items that can be hung in trees to discourage birds from feeding on the fruit. Try using, a ball of crumpled up aluminum foil, empty milk cartons, fake snake, owl or a paper plate with strips of fabric attached. Best to alternate these items since the birds are smart and if they see the same item in the tree all the time they will be back eating the fruit.

PLANT FOOD FOR THE BIRDS
If you plant some of the bird's favorite foods they will leave the rest of the garden and trees alone. These include bayberry, honeysuckle, wild grape, juniper berry, yews, verbena, crab apple, persimmon trees, California poppy, columbine tree, cotoneaster and Virginia creeper.

SPARROWS LOVE APHIDS
If you have a lot of sparrows round your property they should easily take care of any aphid problems you have. Aphids are one of their favorite food sources.

Tetrao parvirostris

BLACKBIRDS

General Information:
Blackbirds include 21 different species of bird with the most common being the red-winged blackbird. They are found throughout the United States and tend to frequent the suburban areas. They are most damaging to cornfields just before harvest time and also love to feast on sunflower heads. While 30% of their diet is insects, which does help, the balance of their diet is usually your corn or berry patch.

BLACKBIRD FACTS
- ➤ The highest breeding densities are to be found in small urban parks and residential areas.
- ➤ The reason for blackbirds success is its adaptability since it is equally at home in a park or suburban garden as it is in a remote forest.
- ➤ Blackbirds are known to be sexually dimorphic, which means that the plumage of the female is completely different from that of the male.
- ➤ The song of the blackbird is the most beautiful any bird, as well as being the most familiar.
- ➤ The first blackbird song of the year is usually heard at the end of January or early February, however, urban birds often start earlier.
- ➤ Blackbirds typically like to sing after rain.
- ➤ Their song period continues well into the summer, but it is unusual to hear sustained songs after the middle of July.
- ➤ The majority of blackbirds seldom move any distance from where they were hatched.
- ➤ The most common causes of death for blackbirds are cats and cars.

- It takes a pair of blackbirds between 11 and 14 days to make a nest with most of the work being done by the female.
- It is only the female that incubates the eggs; however, the male helps feed the offspring.
- The oldest ringed blackbird was over 20 years old.

ROOSTING CONTROL
All trees should be thinned out that are near your garden to reduce their nesting locations. The birds do not feel safe unless they have adequate cover.

AIR-SOCK PEOPLE
The tall "air socks" in the shape of people that you can see around car dealerships will work great to keep blackbirds away. Check with your local car dealership to find out where to purchase them.

BALLOONS TO THE RESCUE
Place some balloons with helium in them and a face painted on the balloon to scare the blackbirds away.

DECOYS WORK GREAT
Owl and hawk decoys will deter these birds without a problem. They are deathly afraid of these birds and will not go near your garden.

SCARE THEM WITH TAPE
You can purchase a bird scare reflecting tape in garden supply stores. Place long strips of the reflecting tape on poles around your garden. When the breezes blow the tape moves and the reflection scares the birds away. Twist the tape before attaching it to the poles to be more effective. It also makes a weird humming noise that scares them off.

TRY A TAPE RECORDER
If you tape the sounds of human voices or a tractor, etc. and place it in your garden it will scare the birds off.

NYLON NETTING WILL BOTHER THEM
There is special thin nylon netting that can be placed over your garden to deter birds that works very well. Check with your local garden supply or hardware store.

CROWS

General Information:
These are one of the smartest birds around and you may have to try a few different methods mentioned for blackbirds to keep them at bay. Crows have even been seen using a stick as a tool to dislodge seeds instead of getting their beaks in the dirt. Crows will eat 600 different types of crops, insects  and foods of every kind imaginable, even road kill. Corn, however, is their favorite food and crows will ignore scarecrows so don't even bother with them. Try all the methods mentioned for blackbirds, but alternate methods since they catch on fast.

Might try the Internet for a CrowBeGone CD to scare them away, sometimes it works and other times it doesn't.

PIGEONS

General Information:
The first images of pigeons that were found by archaeologists were in Mesopotamia (modern Iraq) and dated back to 3000 BC. It was the Sumerians in Mesopotamia that started to breed white doves from the wild pigeons that are common in our towns and cities today, which accounts for the variety of colors that are found in the average flock of urban pigeons.

The first biblical reference to pigeons was in the Old Testament of the Bible in the first millennium BC and was in the story of Noah and the dove of peace.

Later, in the New Testament, the pigeon was even mentioned during the baptism of Christ where the dove descended as the Holy Spirit, an image now used extensively in Christian art.

Pigeon poop is seen as a major problem for property owners of today, however, it was considered to be a valuable resource in the 16th, 17th and 18th century in Europe as a highly prized fertilizer and more effective than farmyard manure. In 16th century England armed guards were stationed at the entrances to pigeon houses to stop thieves from poop stealing.

During modern times the pigeon has been used very effectively during wartime and in both the first and second World Wars the pigeon saved human lives by carrying messages across enemy lines.

A pigeon can be released hundreds of miles away from its home and still return within the day. This feat does not just apply to 'racing' or 'homing' pigeons, all pigeons possess the ability to return to their roost.

Pigeons are one of the most intelligent of all the bird species. A team of navy researchers found that pigeons can be trained to save human lives at sea with high success rates. The navy has trained a number of pigeons to identify red or yellow life jackets (pigeons see colors like humans do) that were floating in the water. The pigeons were found to be more reliable than humans and were many times faster than humans in spotting survivors from a sinking ship.

HOO! ME THAT'S HOO
This is sure-fire and I use it myself with 100% results. Place a plastic owl with a moveable head so that it moves in the wind and you will never have another pigeon problem. Pigeons are deathly afraid of owls.

SCARED OF THEIR REFLECTION
Almost all birds and especially pigeons hate to see their reflection in a mirror. If you glue down some mirrors so that when a bird or pigeon lands on a flat surface they will see themselves, they will leave immediately.

SEAGULLS

General Information

 Seagulls are a normal feature of coastal towns, and have existed alongside humans for many thousands of years. Herring gulls, lesser and greater black-backed gulls all nest in suburban areas and are for the most part popular with visitors to Island and residential areas alike, though at times people may be concerned about their presence since they do leave a mess on occasion.

Seagulls are nesters and occasionally form large colonies of thousands of birds much to the dismay of residents living near their, sites. However, the cause of the decline in some species of seagull is not yet understood, but could be as a result of a change in their marine environment, including over fishing and seashore pollution. The serious decline of seagulls has led to them being protected by law in some areas.

The seagull is an opportunist species that is quick to learn and ready to take advantage of a variety of food sources. They hunt fish and other sea creatures and will take carrion, discarded food, unprotected food as well as the eggs and chicks of other seabirds. They will obtain substantial food by scavenging and are well-placed to take advantage of waste food in gardens, streets and in a garbage can.

In winter they will follow the plough, picking grubs, earthworms and other insects from the freshly turned earth. Where garden bird feeders are accessible, they will also dominate that food source. Small birds and mammals, such as mice can also be part of their diet.

The seagull may be perceived as aggressive in certain situations, especially when it comes to food. Seagulls are very competitive with fellow gulls for food and for that reason may try to take food before it is thrown or discarded, for example, snatching food from a child's hand is not uncommon. This aggressive behavior generally occurs during the breeding season and only when intrusion is quite close to the nest or young.

SEAGULL FACTS

> Seagulls are very clever. They learn, remember and even pass on behaviors, such as stamping their feet in a group to imitate rainfall and trick earthworms to come to the surface.

> Seagulls' intelligence is clearly demonstrated by a range of different feeding behaviors, such as dropping hard-shelled mollusks onto rocks so that they break open so they can eat them.

> Seagulls are attentive and caring parents. The male and female pair for life and they take turns incubating the eggs and feeding and protecting the chicks.

> Gulls have a complex and highly developed repertoire for communication which includes a range of vocalizations and body movements.

> Seagulls can drink both fresh and salt water. Most animals are unable to do this, but seagulls have a special pair of glands right above their eyes which is specifically designed to flush the salt from their systems through openings in the bill.

> A small claw halfway up their lower leg enables them to sit and roost on high ledges without being blown off.

> Young gulls form nursery flocks where they will play and learn vital skills for adulthood.

> Nursery flocks are watched over by a few adult males and these flocks will remain together until the birds are old enough to breed.

> Many seagulls have learned to conserve energy by hovering over bridges in order to absorb raising heat from paved roadways.

> Seagulls are fondly remembered in Utah for helping Mormon settlers deal with a plague of crickets. The seagull is now the state bird of Utah and a monument in Salt Lake City commemorates the event, known as the "Miracle of the Gulls".

SPIKE THE GULL

A humane method of keeping seagulls off your property is with the use of spikes. Where nesting gulls are not wanted on a roof, measures to prevent them nesting may be necessary. The most effective measures involve removing all available food and reducing the attractiveness of nest sites by using physical barriers placed on roofs.

This is not an instant solution and requires planning, the commitment of the building owner and action well ahead of the nesting season. Bird spikes that easily attach to any surface are available at most farm supply stores.

EAGLES WORK, OWLS DON'T!
Plastic eagles on a rooftop have been very effective in some areas and are an inexpensive method and worth trying. If you can find one with a moveable head, it will work better than a stationary one.

GO SUPERSONIC!
Scare away seagulls from your boat or marina with a product designed for boating, called the "Bird Chase Supersonic," which is a speaker system that features 22 different bird distress calls. Also, The Gull Chaser of colored marine ropes and flags attaches to your boat and is specially designed to keep the birds away.

WORKS 100% OF THE TIME
Protect outdoor dining areas with a combination of vertical poles and mono filament lines that is set up over the targeted area. This system keeps the seagulls from landing and roosting while your guests or customers are enjoying lunch on your patio. Check out the Seagull Control systems website for more information.

STARLINGS

General Information:
The first starlings were introduced into North America from England in 1890 by Eugene Schieffelin.

He was determined to introduce all of the animals mentioned in the works of William Shakespeare to North America. A number of the attempts failed, the starling was very successful. The original 100 birds that were introduced are now responsible for the hundreds of millions who live in the U.S. today.

These are real pests and will chase away the good birds and even take over their nests and birdhouses. A flock of starlings can devastate a garden in a short period of time before you even know what happened.

191

Their favorite foods are cherries, blueberries and grapes. However, they will eat fruits and seeds if the berries are not available. They can be found all over the United States and Southern Canada.

Starlings will fly 10-15 miles away from their roosting areas in their daily hunt for food. They are also attracted to livestock areas and will eat their feed and water. Many of the same methods used for blackbirds will also work very well.

STARLING FACTS

> - Starlings have become widespread throughout all of North America and are very common in cities.
> - A starling's song is quite complex and includes a series of whistling notes, chatter and a clear "wolf" whistle.
> - Starlings are members of a family of birds, which include vocal mimics known as myna birds.
> - They are adept at exploiting urban, suburban and agricultural areas.
> - They are one of only a few birds that will put up with areas of high humane density and noise.
> - Starlings have wide-ranging food tolerances, however, they prefer insects.
> - In the spring flocks of starlings will descend on lawns and upset homeowners, who feel they are doing damage when all they are interested in is consuming insect pests and actually doing the homeowners a big favor.
> - It is not unusual to see starlings around dumps and landfills and their specialty is in picking through open dumpsters and trash bags.
> - Starlings usually always flock together when feeding. When traveling, the flock looks like it rolls since the birds at the back of the flock keep moving over and replacing the birds at the front. When a hawk appears, the flock pulls close together to repel a possible attack.
> - Male and female starlings are very similar looking.
> - Both are shiny black with purple and green iridescence on their head, back and breast.
> - Starlings are cavity nesters and will exploit any opening into a suitably sized interior cavity. Some of their favorite sites include dryer, range and bathroom vents.
> - Large flocks of starlings have been known to join with blackbirds at certain times of the year and cause serious problems to agriculture.

- The biggest issue with starlings in urban and suburban areas has to do with their nesting habits. Starling nests built into any house cavity can cause an accumulation of material that is unsightly and could result in the cause of a fire hazard.
- Starlings never remove material from old nests but keep adding year after year to what is there.
- Starlings cause problems by getting into trash, competing with "desirable" birds at feeders and tend to get stuck in chimneys and metal flues.

STICK-'EM-UP

There is a product called Roost No More™, which can be placed on ledges and other areas that they will make their nest on. Tanglefoot™ also works well as a deterrent if you smear it along areas that they may roost on.

THEY WILL GET BOARD

If you place a board at a 45^0 angle on any ledges it will stop them from making a nest. If you keep a bright light in areas where they may nest it will also discourage them.

AVOID A POSSIBLE FIRE DANGER

Dryer and range vents must be screened with hardware cloth or other screening material since this is one of the starlings favorite place to nest.

SCARE 'EM AWAY

Try both visual and auditory scare devices both of which can be effective. Pie tins or party balloons hung out in the garden can also be very effective. There are also a number of commercial products that are available at your farmer's supply stores.

SCARE TAPE

This is strong, laminated metal and plastic material that was originally designed for use in the space program. It is very reflective and creates a dizzying pattern of light when in motion. There are various types available including one that makes noise in the wind and combines visual and auditory stimuli. Best to cut into strips of varying lengths and widths, this tape can be attached to posts, wires, gutters on houses or anywhere else to repel the birds.

SCARE BALOONS

These rely on what is called a "supernormal" stimulus and incorporates a highly enhanced "eye" that is located in the center of the balloon. Yellow, black and white styles are made, however, yellow seems to be the most effective. They are suspended from a support or sometimes even filled with helium; these balloons move in the slightest wind and are very effective. Both Scare Tape and Scare Balloons are available from Bird-X™. Their products are safe for animals and for the environment.

ATTACK OF THE BERRY EATERS

If you have a serious problem in your area, you will have to place netting over all berry bushes on poles, held down with rocks around the edges. Starlings will go to extreme lengths to get berries.

WOODPECKERS

General Information

The pileated woodpecker is the largest North American woodpecker.

Woodpeckers are instantly recognizable by their unique behavior of pecking vertically on trees, houses and poles. There are more than 180 species of woodpeckers worldwide, but none are found in Australia, Madagascar or New Zealand.

The downy woodpecker is the most common woodpecker in North America and is one of only about 24 woodpecker species found in the United States. The most common feather colors for all woodpeckers are black, white, red and yellow. A few of the species also have orange, green, brown, maroon and gold in their coloration.

A woodpecker's tongue can be as long as 4 inches depending on the species and it wraps around the skull. Many species of woodpeckers have barbed tongues that help them remove bugs from trees and holes. Most woodpeckers have "zygodactyl" feet; which means they have toes facing both the front and back to help them grip trees and poles vertically. They use those toes and stiff tail feathers to brace themselves on trees as they climb.

Woodpeckers; main diet is bugs, sap, fruit, nuts and seeds. In the backyard, they are often attracted to suet feeders or nut feeders.
The two largest woodpeckers in the world are the imperial woodpecker and the ivory-billed woodpecker, but both are possibly extinct. The largest confirmed woodpecker is the great slaty woodpecker of Southeast Asia, which measures 20 inches long.

The piculets are a member of the woodpecker family and are found in South America and Asia and are the smallest woodpeckers, measuring only 3-4 inches long depending on the species.

Woodpeckers do not sing and instead they drum on resonant objects such as hollow trees and logs, utility poles, chimneys, rain gutters and trash cans. This woodpecker drumming is necessary to attract mates, establish territories and communicate.

WOODPECKER FACTS

> Between feeding, excavating nests and drumming, woodpeckers can peck up to 20 times per second, or a total of 8,000-12,000 pecks per day.
> Woodpeckers never get headaches from pecking since they have reinforced skulls structured to spread the impact force and their brains are tightly cushioned and protected.
> Most woodpeckers have a very distinct undulating flight consisting of a few rapid wing beats then followed by a quick glide when the wings are tucked against the body rather than spread like many other birds.
> The average life span of a wild woodpecker can last from 5-11 years, depending on the species.
> The greatest threat to woodpeckers include habitat loss through urban development and overpopulation, insecticide use that eliminates food sources and natural disasters such as forest fires that eliminate dead wood for feeding and nesting.
> Pileated woodpeckers may spend up to 30 days carving out an oval-shaped nesting cavity.
> During nesting season, male pileated woodpeckers may spend 18 hours a day incubating eggs.
> Most woodpeckers have some red on their heads, but the red-headed woodpecker is the only one with a completely red head.

- Red-headed woodpeckers have been known to chisel nesting cavities up to 24 inches deep in tall trees, but they'll nest in man-made birdhouses as well.
- Woodpeckers can do a lot of damage and can be a real pest. They are usually after carpenter bees and tend to look for their tunnels.

VINEGAR DOES THE TRICK

To discourage the woodpeckers from digging into the holes looking for bugs, just spray a solution of 2 tablespoons of white vinegar mixed in 1 quart of water into the holes or around the areas they frequent.

CHAPTER 6

BENEFICIAL CRITTERS

BATS

General Information:
Bats love night-flying insects and consume them voraciously. They locate their prey through *"echolocation."* The bat sends out sounds waves similar to sonar and then interprets them to locate the bug. Bats are the only mammals capable of flight.

A colony of 200,000 bats will consume about 3 tons of insects every night. They are also involved in pollinating plants and helping to disperse seeds. Birds eat the insects that are awake during the day and bats go to work at night where the birds left off. Since mosquitoes are active at night and one bat can eat about 4,000 mosquitoes, try to be nice to them, especially when they live in your neighborhood.

Bats never attack people and only get near people when they need water. If you are in your pool at night they may come in for a drink but will then leave as soon as they have had their fill.

LIGHTING UP THE BATS
If you have a bat problem in your attic, just place few lights up there and they will vacate the attic in short order and never some back.

FAN THE BATS
An attic fan will disturb the bats to such a degree that they will move to someone else's attic. Even a draft of cool air will cause them not to roost since they need a calm air, quiet, dark location.

We love bats!

Yum! Gourmet bugs

BATS IN THE HOUSE

If a bat gets into the house, try not to panic since they are very gentle creatures and only want to get back out. Just close the bat off in one room and open a window in that room. When the bat feels the current of air it will immediately leave the premises.

GET A BAT HOUSE

There is an organization for bats and you can contact them regarding building or purchasing a bat house. They are called Bat Conservation International (BCI) and the house is designed especially for bats. The bat houses need to be located near a body of water or swimming pool and on a tree trunk about 20+ feet high.

FERRETS

General Information:

 Ferrets are a natural hunter and can be a real asset around the garden. They were brought to the United States from Europe where they were a **"working animal."** They would prowl shipyards, warehouses and farms eliminating rats and mice. They are related to minks, weasels and otters. They can even be trained to walk on a leash or ride on your shoulder. If you want one for a hunter get a females called **"jills"** since they are not as lazy as the males. They need to be fed mice and some commercial pet food. It is best to get them when they are babies and train them.

They are not good diggers but if placed into a tunnel they will clear any animal out in short order. Gophers, moles and rabbits do not like ferrets.

SKINKS

General Information

 The distinctive marked striped skink is one of the least known and rarely seen lizards. The species is easily recognizable by the stripes running down the length of its body and makes for an eye-catching sight with its lightening quick movements. The striped skink is listed as "endangered."

All the species of skinks found in Florida prowl on the ground for small insects, although the larger species also climb trees and wooden structures. The skink family is a large group and this lizard is found on all continents. Larger skinks may try to bite but a skink will rarely break the skin. Many skinks have blue tails, which is part of a defense strategy called "defective coloration." The blue color is supposed to serve as a warning to predators that the skink is poisonous and there is some actual evidence that the blue tails are poisonous if eaten.

Some of the various species of skink found in the United States are as follows:

Southeastern Five-lined Skink

These are moderately large lizards that have short legs and a streamlined body. Their body is generally gray, brown, or black, in background color with five white or yellowish stripes down the center of the back. The young have a bright blue tail, however, the adult males' stripes may fade and a reddish or orange coloration may develop on its head. This species of skink may be found on the ground or in trees, but are generally less of a tree dweller than broadhead skinks.

Although sometimes seen in the open, these lizards are most often found beneath logs or under tree bark. If you pursue these lizards, they will generally run for the nearest tree or log and can be quite difficult to capture similar to many other lizards, southeastern five-lined skinks will break off their tails when restrained, distracting the predator and allowing the lizard to escape.

Ground Skink

These are relatively small, slender lizards with long tails and short legs. They range in color from golden brown to almost black in but are most often coppery brown with a darker stripe running along each side of their body and their belly is white or yellowish. Like many other lizards that make their home in Florida, ground skinks never climb. Instead of running on their tiny legs, ground skinks use their slender bodies to wriggle or "swim" through leaf litter or loose soil and can disappear in a flash as soon as they are discovered.

Mole Skinks

These are small, thin lizards with long tails and short legs. They range from grayish to brown in background color with two light stripes running along each side of their body and have a red or orange tail that never fades with age. This is the only lizard in Florida with a red tail and this easily distinguishes them from the similar ground skink. These lizards are very good at burrowing and prefer areas of loose sandy soil. They generally would prefer hot and dry habitats, which is different from the similar ground skink and are often found beneath leaf litter, logs, boards, and other cover objects.

Mole skinks are probably the most common in sandy scrub and coastal dune habitats and often live on offshore islands. Instead of running on their tiny legs, mole skinks tend to wriggle or "swim" through sand or loose soil. Mole skinks are so secretive that a lot remains to be learned about their habits and behavior. The Key West Mole Skink is currently endangered. They eat tiny insects, spiders, and other invertebrates. The female ground skinks lay several eggs in moist soil or rotten logs during the summer. It is also suspected that ground skinks may lay several clutches per season.

Broad Headed Skink

These skinks have long been called scorpions by uninformed rural southerners who believe that they are venomous. The males during the breeding season have bright orange head coloration and the heads of large males are much larger than those of females. Their head remains red throughout the breeding period in May and June; however, it fades by July. Broadheaded skinks are active foragers that move through the habitat looking for small animal prey and will on occasion eat fruit such as blackberries, raspberries and grapes.

While foraging they will flick their tongues out frequently to locate scents of prey. They eat a wide range of small invertebrates, especially insects, many of which are found under logs or surface litter on the forest floor.

Florida Sand Skink

This is one of the most highly adapted scrub creatures, the 4 inch sand skink occurs nowhere in the world except six counties in central Florida. Similar to most members of the skink family, the sand skink is a smooth-scaled, shiny lizard that prefers to stay out of sight. The sand skink is on the U.S. list of Threatened species. They are very vulnerable to extinction because of habitat loss as more and more of the Florida scrub is cleared for development.

It is a unique lizard adapted to an underground existence. The sand skink measures 4 to 5 inches in length and has a gray to tan color. It has a wedge-shaped head, a partially countersunk lower jaw, body grooves into which the forelegs can be folded and tiny eyes which have transparent windows in the lower lids. These features enable the lizard to swim beneath the surface of loose sand. The diet of the Florida Mole Skink consists of surface-dwelling invertebrates, which include beetle larvae and termites.

SKINK FACTS
- Striped skinks give birth in summer and can have up to eight young in a litter.
- Growth rates and lifespan are unknown, but an adult in captivity has lived for over 20 years.
- Their diet in the wild is usually small insects and they love termites. In captivity they mainly eat insects, but will also eat soft fruit.
- Skinks are found in mature lowland forest and pastoral farmland as well as in Florida.
- The striped skink is a good climber and may spend most of its time in the canopy of mature forest.
- Skinks have been known to live beneath flaking bark and crevasses in trunks as well as tree branches. They also dwell in logs and litter on the forest floor. On farmland they tend to live in rotting logs or rank vegetation. Striped skinks have also been found in swampland.
- Striped skinks have been shown to have high rates of evaporative water loss making them susceptible to dehydration.

TOADS

General Information:

Approximately 90% of the toad's diet is insects and the majority of them are pests that will damage your garden. There are 18 species of toads in the United States and all species are beneficial to man. Ponds will attract them and should be kept up in good order to keep them around. Toads do give off a noxious substance when handled and you should wash after touching one.

Toads never drink through their mouth but absorb moisture through their skin. The female toad can deposit as many as 25,000 eggs, which turn into tadpoles.

DON'T KISS A TOAD

Finding a toad in your garden is really good luck but you don't have to kiss it. A single toad will feast on over 100 slugs and snails, cutworms, grubs, caterpillars and an assortment of beetles and their larvae.

If you are lucky enough to have a really big, healthy toad in top physical condition (one that works out) it can consume over 10,000 invaders in one season.

TURTLES

General Information:

Wood turtles and box turtles are the most common turtle that people find visiting their gardens in search of snails and slugs. They may also be interested in low-lying berry patches. They do more good than damage and should be tolerated. If you have a garden pool or pond they will become regular visitors.

If you have frogs in your area, it would be best to make them as comfortable as possible by making them a home from an inverted clay pot with a hole in it and leave some water nearby.

Small wasps called "braconids" can be purchased to sting and kill caterpillars and other similar pests. However, poisons used in the garden will kill a lot of natural predators as well as the pests.

APPENDIX A

PLANTS THAT REPEL PESTS

PEST	PLANT
Cats	Rue
Dogs	Marigolds
Deer	Gambel oak, fourwing saltbush,

Rocky Mountain smooth sumac, Saskatoon serviceberry, and Wood's rose. There are a number of plants that deer won't eat unless they're absolutely starving: blue spruce, hawthorn, holly, Norway maple, smoke tree, walnut, boxwood, butterfly bush, mountain mahogany, junipers, potentilla, redtwig dogwood, rhododendron, scotch broom, wild lilac, lily of the valley, dianthus, peppermint and spearmint, St. John's wort, clematis, English ivy, bee balm, daffodils, daylilies, echinacea, dusty miller, coreopsis, foxglove, iris, lamb's ear, oregano, oriental poppy, pampass grass, sword fern, yarrow, and hen's and chicks.

Gopher	Castor bean
Mice	Mint
Mole	Spurge, castor bean, mole plant,
Rabbit	Allium family
Rats	Mint

APPENDIX B

DANGEROUS FOOD & PLANTS
FOR DOGS & CATS

I am sure that at times, as pet owners we have at times thought we were giving our pets a treat by feeding them human foods, which were really not good for them. However, it has been difficult to know, which foods we should not be feeding them that might either make them ill or in some cases even kill them.

Even though some of the following foods are healthy foods, your pet cannot digest them properly. To avoid poisoning your pet or making them sick I am providing this crucial information!

Alcoholic Beverages: All types of alcohol in any form can be poisonous to your pet and can coma or even death if enough is consumed.

Apple Seeds: Contain cyanide and even a small amount may be harmful.

Apricot Pits: Contains cyanide and may cause breathing difficulties as well as coughing and even sneezing.

Cherry Pits: Contains cyanide and can cause breathing problems, coughing and sneezing.

Candy containing the artificial sweetener Xylitol: May cause liver damage and even death.

Cat Food: Too high in protein for most dogs.

Chocolate: Theobromine contained in chocolate is dangerous to cats and dogs and is a cardiac stimulant and a diuretic. Never give pets any type of chocolate! Milk chocolate will not be as dangerous for animals as dark chocolate, semi-sweet or unsweetened bakers chocolate. Symptoms of chocolate poisoning include irregular heart rate and arrhythmia, restlessness, hyperactivity, diarrhea, vomiting, uncontrolled panting, muscle tremors, stomach discomfort, bloody stools and urine, fever, seizures and even death.

Coffee: May result in increased respiration and fast heart rate, restlessness and has a negative effect on the nervous system.

Garlic: Contains thiosulphate, but would take large amounts to cause problems.

Eggs (raw): Contain an enzyme called avidin, which can decrease the absorption of biotin (B vitamin). This may lead to skin and hair coat problems.

Fish (raw): May result in a thiamine (B vitamin) deficiency leading to loss of appetite, seizures and even death. This is a higher risk if raw fish is fed regularly.

Grapes: A large amounts of white or red grapes can be poisonous to pets and can cause lack of energy, vomiting, diarrhea, stomach discomfort, lack of appetite and kidney damage.

Hops, Beer: May cause increase in respiration, fever, increased heart rate, seizures and possibly death.

Macadamia Nuts: One of the worst nuts to give a pet! May cause vomiting, lack of energy, fever, stomach discomfort, joint problems and muscle tremors.

Moldy Foods: May cause vomiting and diarrhea depending on the type of mold.

Milk & Dairy Foods: Some adult dogs and cats may not have sufficient amounts of the enzyme lactase and may be deficient. This can result in diarrhea. Try lactose-free milk products for pets

Mushrooms: Best not to ever give a pet mushrooms since different varieties will have negative effects on different breeds of pets. Symptoms can include loss of energy, diarrhea, nausea and vomiting, stomach discomfort, loss of bowel control, liver failure, seizures, uncontrolled urination, kidney failure, heart damage and in some cases, death.

Mustard Seeds: May have different effects depending on the breed.

Onions and Onion Powder: Contain the chemical thiosulphate and may cause gastrointestinal discomfort and diarrhea.

Peach Pits: Contains cyanide and may cause breathing problems, coughing and sneezing.

Potato Leaves and Stems: May cause digestive and urinary system problems.

Raisins: A large quantity of raisins may be poisonous to pets and may cause vomiting, diarrhea, lack of energy, stomach discomfort, loss of appetite and kidney damage.

Rhubarb Leaves: The leaves are poisonous to pets as well as humans. Problems can include digestive disorders, nervous and urinary system upsets.

Salt: A large quantity may cause sodium/potassium electrolyte imbalances

Tea: Certain teas may have different effects in varied breeds.

Tomato Leaves and Stems: May cause problems with the gastrointestinal, nervous and urinary systems.

Walnuts: May cause gastrointestinal problems to include vomiting and diarrhea, breathing problems and coughing.

Yeast Dough: May be dangerous since it will expand and result in flatulence, stomach discomfort and could even rupture the stomach or intestines.

TOXIC PLANTS

If your dog is allowed to roam outside then there are a number of toxic plants you should be aware of. Certain plants are actually poisonous to our pets.

POINSETTIAS
While these are probably very popular holiday plants with either red, white or pink leaves, they contain a milky irritant sap and could induce vomiting, loss of appetite and even depression.

LILLY FAMILY
Some members of the lily family may result in serious illness in cats. Ones to be careful of are Easter lilies, tiger lilies and Japanese show lilies. Some hybrids and day lilies have been known to cause kidney failure.

SPECIAL NOTE:
If you have any suspicion in the slightest that you're pet has consumed any of the above product or has been poisoned, contact the American Society for the Prevention of Cruelty to Animals (ASPCA) Poison Control Center at 1-888-426-4435. This number is a 24 hour a day hotline.

APPENDIX C

REMOVING A SKUNK SMELL FROM DOGS

Removing skunk spray from a dog will take some patience from both the pet owner and the pet. The odor can be masked using tomato juice or apple cider vinegar, but that only masks it! The spray from skunks is very oily and contains sulfur. You will need to break up the oil plus neutralize the odor for a successful removal.

If you live in an area that skunks frequent, it would be best if you were always prepared for the worst and not wait until it happens to obtain the ingredients needed to resolve the problem.

Ingredients needed:
Rubber latex gloves
Small strips of eye lubricant (Puralube™)
Mineral oil
Plastic bucket
Plastic sheet, size depending on the dog's size
1 Quart hydrogen peroxide (H_2O_2)
2 teaspoons liquid soap
$\frac{1}{4}$ Cup baking soda

Instructions:
1. Place the plastic sheet between you and the dog
2. Put on the rubber gloves and check for eye redness or discharge
3. If any injury is found, take the dog to the vet as soon as you clean them, immediately if the injury is severe
4. The time element is important and the cleaning needs to be started immediately
5. Best to do the cleaning outdoors
6. Apply a small strip of eye lubricant or 1-2 drops of mineral oil in your dog's eyes to protect the eyes in case any of the solution splashes or drips in.

7. In the plastic bucket, combine 1 quart hydrogen peroxide, ¼ cup baking soda and 2 teaspoons of liquid soap.
8. Add enough lukewarm water as needed for large dogs.
9. Mix ingredients well. The peroxide solution should fizz since it is a chemical reaction then use immediately and do not store the remainder of the solution
10. Do not soak your dog with water prior to the bath and begin cleansing the affected areas immediately and thoroughly, massaging the solution deep into your dog's coat with a sponge or washcloth. Try not to get the solution in the eyes, ears or mouth
11. Allow the solution to remain on your dog for at least five minutes or longer if strong odor persists
12. Rinse your dog with lukewarm water
13. Repeat another cleaning if necessary until odor is gone
14. Dry your dog well and give her a treat! A BIGGGG TREAT!

IMPORTANT NOTE:

➤ **NEVER** place the solution in a closed container or spray bottle since as the pressure will build up and the container could burst. This could cause serious injury to you and your dog.
➤ **NEVER** use higher concentrations of hydrogen peroxide or substitute baking soda with A **SIMILAR** products. The altered chemical reaction may cause severe injury to you and your dog.
➤ **ALWAYS** use fresh hydrogen peroxide since it becomes less concentrated over time and will lose its effectiveness.

The solution can be used to remove skunk odor from clothing and other fabrics. Be aware that the solution can have a mild bleaching effect on some materials. In addition, your dog's coat may become slightly lighter as a result of the solution. If this happens, it should resolve over time.

CATS

Cats may be more of a problem than dogs since most cats hate water. You may have to have assistance or place the cat in a carrier and try to work within it as best you can. **GOOD LUCK WITH CATS!**

APPENDIX D

CATALOGS OF PEST CONTROL PRODUCTS

Gardener's Supply
128 Intervale Road
Burlington, VT 05401

Harmony Farm Supply
3244 Gravenstein Hwy North
Sebastopol, CA 95472

Solutions
P.O. Box 6878
Portland, OR 97228-6878

Maag Agrochemicals Inc.
5699 Kings Hwy.
Vero Beach, FL 32961-6430
Fire ant baits

PLANT NETTING
Orchard Supply Co.
P.O. Box 956
Sacramento, CA 95805

SCARY BALLOONS
Rid-A-Bird Inc.
P.O. Box 436
Wilton, IA 52778

GOPHER TRAPS
Guardian Trap Co.
P.O. Box 1935
San Leandro, CA 94577

Gurney's
110 Capital St.
Yankton, SD 57079

Mellinger's
2310 W. South Range Rd.
North Lima, OH 44452-9731

Unique Insect Control
5504 Sperry Dr.
Citrus Heights, CA 95621

Bat Conservation Intern.
P.O. Box 162603
Austin, TX 78716-2603
Bat house plans

Animal Repellants Inc.
P.O. Box 999
Griffin, GA 30224

GLUE BOARDS
J.T. Eaton & Co.
1393 Highland Rd.
Twinsburg, OH 44087

INDEX